"Dr. Gujrathi's voice is exactly what the next generation of leaders needs—clear, compassionate, and deeply wise. *The Mirror Effect* is more than a book; it's a call to evolve how we lead and how we live."

Marci Shimoff, #1 *New York Times*–bestselling author of *Happy for No Reason* and *Chicken Soup for the Woman's Soul*

"Stepping into one's true potential can feel like an abstract goal until you encounter Dr. Gujrathi's framework. This book is the practical, empathetic manual for anyone ready to stop chasing external validation and start building their own table."

Selena Rezvani, author of the *Wall Street Journal* bestseller *Quick Confidence: Be Authentic, Boost Connections, and Make Bold Bets on Yourself*

"*The Mirror Effect* is a powerful guide to designing a career and life with intention. Dr. Sheila Gujrathi blends personal insight with behavioral science to help marginalized leaders reclaim their agency and thrive on their own terms. Bold, actionable, and deeply needed."

Nir Eyal, bestselling author of *Indistractable*

"*The Mirror Effect* is a compelling and courageous call to action for women leaders who have long been expected to shrink themselves to fit in. Dr. Sheila Gujrathi offers a thoughtful framework rooted in authenticity, inclusion, and empowerment. By sharing her journey and the collective strength of the Biotech CEO Sisterhood and SABA, she provides a roadmap to help underrepresented leaders find their voice, build strong support systems, and thrive in spaces that need transformation."

Kiran Mazumdar-Shaw, executive chairperson, Biocon, and pioneering global biotechnology entrepreneur

"*The Mirror Effect* is a transformational guide for high-achieving women and marginalized leaders ready to break free from roles that no longer serve them and dismantle the inner glass ceiling shaped by fear, doubt, and systemic conditioning. Through hard-earned wisdom, vivid archetypes, and deeply personal reflection, Dr. Gujrathi helps you reclaim your power by seeing yourself, the leader you already are, more clearly and building a career on your own terms."

Kelli Thompson, award-winning executive coach, speaker, and author of *Closing the Confidence Gap*

"Dr. Gujrathi provides a rare, unfiltered perspective on the corporate world, offering suggestions that transcend gender. Her insights on building a robust support network are invaluable for anyone looking to navigate the professional landscape."

Jayant Sinha, president, Eversource Capital, and former Union Minister, Government of India

"In *The Mirror Effect*, Dr. Sheila Gujrathi will help you shed the masks you've worn to 'fit in' so you can confidently step into your unique genius. This book guides you on a path to make a life and career worth mirroring. Bravo!

Stephen "Shed" Shedletzky, speaker, coach, and author of *Speak-Up Culture*

amplify
an imprint of Amplify Publishing Group

www.amplifypublishinggroup.com

The Mirror Effect: A Transformative Approach to Growth
for the Next Generation of Female Leaders

For more information, please contact:
Amplify Publishing, an imprint of Amplify Publishing Group
620 Herndon Parkway, Suite 220
Herndon, VA 20170
info@amplifypublishing.com

Library of Congress Control Number: 2025909236

CPSIA Code: PRV0725A

ISBN-13: 979-8-89138-595-5

Printed in the United States

To JSJ, my family, and all my sisters and brothers who have shown me kindness on my life journey. You have been my mirrors, for which I am forever grateful.

DR. SHEILA GUJRATHI

the
MIRROR
EFFECT

amplify
an imprint of Amplify Publishing Group

A TRANSFORMATIVE APPROACH *to* GROWTH *for the* NEXT GENERATION *of* FEMALE LEADERS

"You alone are enough. You have nothing to prove to anybody."

–Maya Angelou

CONTENTS

PART III: MAKE A LIFE WORTH MIRRORING: SET YOURSELF UP FOR SUCCESS

A LETTER TO YOU

Dear Reader,

I want to start by holding up a mirror for you. Imagine you're looking into the glass and seeing your true brilliance reflected back at you, not the distorted image you may have carried for years. That's the goal of this book, though I know from personal experience that it doesn't come easily.

For most of my life, I operated from a place of fear disguised as ambition. Like so many women, immigrants, people of color, and other historically marginalized groups, I spent decades trying to fit into environments that weren't designed for me. I changed how I spoke, what I ate, even how I laughed—anything to belong.

I endured bullying and microaggressions while smiling and saying "thank you." I became a master people-pleaser, convinced that if I just worked hard enough, proved myself enough, I'd finally be worthy of a seat at the table.

The irony didn't appear to me until deep into my career, when I'd racked up accomplishments and accolades and board seats: I was already worthy. I always had been. But it took me years to realize that the voice driving my success—that relentless inner critic demanding I prove myself over and over—was the same voice holding me back from true fulfillment.

This awakening didn't happen overnight. It began when I started questioning why, despite my achievements, I still felt like I was performing rather than living. Why I prioritized everyone else's comfort over my own well-being. Why I embraced "servant leadership" to the point of self-sacrifice. The revelation that changed everything was this: I had to learn to have my own back.

Having your own back means believing in yourself even when others don't. It means respecting yourself enough to walk away from toxic situations. It means understanding that putting yourself first isn't selfish; it's necessary for authentic leadership and genuine happiness. This shift transformed not just my work life but every aspect of how I move through the world.

That's why I wrote this book. We need to see our brilliance reflected back to us until we can finally see it ourselves. Over the years, I've learned so many lessons, some of them painful. I want to impart those lessons while sparing you some of the pain. I got stuck being comfortable being uncomfortable for years, but you don't have to suffer as I did.

In these pages, I'll challenge you to confront the deepest parts of yourself—the fear, insecurity, doubt, and shame that may be running the show behind the scenes. You'll learn to identify the limiting archetypes you've been playing and discover how to break through your inner glass ceiling. I'll ask you to examine toxic work environments with new eyes, teaching you to distinguish between your reactions and others' projections. You'll discover how to read difficult personalities—the tyrants, rivals, and deceivers—with compassion while protecting your own energy and boundaries.

Most importantly, you'll learn practical tools for transformation: how to build a personal board of directors who truly see you, how to negotiate from a place of strength rather than desperation, and how to manage your energy so you show up as your most powerful self. These aren't just concepts—they're battle-tested strategies I've used and taught to hundreds of leaders who've gone on to create extraordinary careers and lives.

This book is divided into three parts that mirror a journey:

- Hold Up Your Own Mirror: Know Thyself
- Reflect on Your Surroundings: Understand Your Environment
- Make a Life Worth Mirroring: Set Yourself Up for Success

I hope you'll read it chapter by chapter and then return as needed, revisiting the content like you would an old friend who knows you better than you know yourself. Come back with challenges in mind, looking for the advice necessary to trudge ahead. It will always be here for you. The landscape of your life and the world may change, but the mirror will meet you wherever you are.

If you want to go deeper, my companion workbook and journal is designed to walk alongside you as you read and process the information shared here. It's broken into ninety exercises: thirty focused on deep self-reflection, thirty on environmental awareness, and thirty on powerful action. Use the workbook and journal to capture your insights, work through the exercises, and—most importantly—to practice having your own back. Write down your wins, your struggles, and your realizations. Let it become a conversation between who you've been and who you're becoming.

I've also learned the importance and power of peer groups and communities. Consider reading this book and completing the workbook and journal with a friend, peer group, or book club. It's a great way to create accountability and grow together. Meanwhile, I'm right here with you every step of the way like a good friend, trusted colleague, mentor, and sponsor—someone who believes in you even when your confidence flags.

You are powerful beyond measure. You always have been. Now it's time to live like you believe it.

With love, compassion, and solidarity,

Sheila

P.S. For more insight on how the Mirror Effect came to be, check out my TEDx Talk, "Shattering the Glass Ceiling by Finding the Right Mirrors," where I first shared this concept.

Elevate Your Experience with the Companion Workbook & Journal

You're embarking on a powerful journey with *The Mirror Effect*. To maximize its impact and personalize your transformation as you read, we've built *The Mirror Effect Workbook & Journal: Growth Exercises for the Next Generation of Female Leaders.*

It's designed to be used alongside the main book, providing ninety days of powerful prompts that help you apply insights, reflect on your personal and professional identity, and actively chart a course toward your most authentic and empowered self.

Scan this QR code to purchase from Amplify's bookstore, or check your favorite online and local booksellers.

PART I

HOLD UP YOUR OWN MIRROR: KNOW THYSELF

CHAPTER 1

IT'S TIME
Reclaiming Your Vision and Voice

"It took me quite a long time to develop a voice, and now that I have it, I am not going to be silent."

–Madeleine Albright

My stomach dropped as soon as I read her text:

"Can you talk?"

I'd met Sara several years earlier when I interviewed her for a position at my company. The role wasn't the right fit for her, but she impressed me with her confidence and expertise. While we never worked closely together, we'd supported one another along our career trajectories and developed mutual respect and admiration.

Sara was a talented executive. She worked with prominent investors and sat on multiple boards. She had immense promise, and it was clear that she was well on her way to becoming CEO at her current company. Knowing all of this about her made her text sound extremely ominous, so I cleared my next hour of meetings and called her immediately.

"I need your advice, Sheila," Sara said, then proceeded to describe a delicate situation at work. She was facing some challenges with her boss, and since she knew I'd had similar experiences in the past, she wanted to know how I'd handled them.

Sara's voice shook as she relayed what was happening; she wasn't her usual confident self.

"What's really going on here, Sara?" I asked.

For a moment, there was silence. Then she started to cry.

Through her tears, Sara opened up: Her boss, who had been mentoring her and preparing her to step into the CEO role, had completely changed his behavior. She felt like he was doing everything possible to undermine her ascent. He'd begun questioning her in meetings, and their previously warm relationship seemed to have gone cold.

The board's attitude toward her had also chilled. So many arrangements were in place for her to advance to CEO, but none of them had been put into writing. It was like a switch had been flipped—everything she had been working toward had gone dark—and Sara blamed herself. But she didn't know why.

"What did I do wrong?" she asked me. She questioned her own skills, wondering if all the great things her boss had said about her in the past had been false. She wasn't sleeping well, replaying every work interaction in her mind, night after night.

After hearing her out, I asked a few questions. Did she feel safe in this environment? Did she have allies at the company?

For the next hour, I counseled Sara, offering wisdom and insight from my own professional experience. I advised her it was time to take action and address the situation. She had to directly ask her boss and the other board members if they would support her in the CEO role. Only then would she know if she was being set up for success. We discussed different tactics Sara could use when interacting with her boss, as well as how to broach difficult conversations with the board.

As our call wound down, I said, "Life is short, Sara. I know how talented you are, and I can guarantee you other opportunities are available with people who share your values. So I'm going to ask you a question, and I don't want you to think too long before answering. Are you excited to go to work every morning, the way you were at the beginning?"

Sara took a moment to think. "Great question," she said. "I need to mull it all over. But right now, my gut says this might not be the best place for my first CEO job after all."

Three months later, she gave that company her notice. Three months after that, she stepped into a CEO role at another company, backed by an amazing group of investors who were over the moon about her joining them. She would get to build her own board and her own team after all—and under much better conditions.

This time, when her text came, I knew the tide had turned. And when I called to congratulate her, I could hear it in her voice: This was the Sara I knew—confident, talented, excited—and she was back on her ascent to tremendous success.

I wish I could say Sara's situation was an isolated incident. But almost every week I receive calls, texts, emails, and messages from highly successful leaders who are struggling. These leaders are often disenfranchised: they are women; people of color; and professionals who are queer, disabled, neurodiverse. Many, like me, are women of color—members of two marginalized groups.

Some are dear friends. Others are acquaintances who track me down through our shared network, or people I've never met who find me on LinkedIn.

"I work hard, but nobody sees me."

"My CEO chastised me for wearing my heart on my sleeve. He said I'm too emotional and need a better poker face."

"I was just passed over for a promotion even though I'm the most-qualified candidate."

These leaders hail from all walks of life. They work in various industries in many different countries, possessing an impressive breadth and depth of expertise. But if you look at each message as a single thread woven into a large and intricate tapestry, you begin to see some common themes—including the double standards so many of us face.

We hear we're not good enough, not right for the role or the promotion and given no clarity as to why. And then, often in the same breath, we're scolded for not believing in ourselves.

We're told we're too emotional, that we need to toughen up—and then we're criticized for having "sharp elbows."

People tell us we'll never reach our goals if we're not more confident, but when we speak up in board meetings, senior leaders at the table swiftly put us in our place.

I know all this from personal experience. I've had a robust career in the biotech and pharmaceutical space, serving as medical director, VP, SVP, CMO, CEO, and board director at multiple small startups and large pharmaceutical companies. I founded and co-founded a few biopharmaceutical companies and currently chair several boards. Over the past twenty years, I've run successful clinical programs and developed new therapies that are treating patients all over the world. Yet I still experience imposter syndrome whenever I take on a new high-powered role. And I'm in good company. A KPMG study found that an astounding 75 percent of executive women just a step or two from the C-suite struggled with imposter syndrome throughout their careers.[1]

But the truth is, the gnawing sense that we don't belong isn't just on us—not at all.

Times Are Changing—but Not Fast Enough

In the wake of social justice movements and a global pandemic that has changed the way we do business, we've seen Corporate America slowly awaken to a fundamental truth: hiring diverse leaders improves business outcomes. A McKinsey & Company report showed that companies in the top quartile for gender diversity on executive teams were 25 percent more likely to have above-average profitability; those in the top quartile for ethnic diversity were 36 percent more profitable.[2] *Harvard Business Review* conducted similar research in the world of venture capital—a space that has not historically been diverse—and saw improved financial performance on both individual investments and overall fund returns.[3] Many organizations have attempted to usher in a pronounced cultural shift and hire candidates from all backgrounds and walks of life.

And yet, so many diverse leaders are still fighting an uphill battle. Those company commitments are often hollow, rolled out for the sake of PR, not because they're actually committed to institutional change. The irony is rich: Even though a genuine commitment to diversity has been linked to positive business incomes, these companies are mired in their old ways. Even those who have shown dedication to supporting leaders from underrepresented groups in the past have felt forced to roll back that support in light of cultural backlash and legislative pressures.

This is partly why historically marginalized leaders feel so disenfranchised. Even when the numbers are in their favor and businesses have every financial incentive to bring in *and nurture* diverse talent, we get sidelined and shoved aside.

Case in point: though we may be seeing better representation for women in high-powered positions, only 8.1 percent of Fortune 500 companies have women CEOs.[4] Just 4 percent of companies have a woman as board chair.[5] According to a *Fortune* study, there are more male chairs named John in the United States than female chairs, total!

A landmark study conducted between 2015 and 2022 by McKinsey and LeanIn.org surveyed more than four hundred thousand women at eight hundred companies, including women of color, queer women, and women with disabilities.[6] The study found an alarming rate of attrition. Women in leadership roles—senior managers and up—are switching jobs at the highest rate in history. That means companies are struggling to retain the relatively small number of women leaders they *do* have. While many people resigned from their jobs during the pandemic in what's been dubbed the "Great Resignation," the report found that women were feeling extra motivated to leave their positions because of toxic environments, discriminatory behavior, and getting passed up for promotions.[7]

Survey participants wanted more opportunity, flexibility, support for employee well-being, and diversity, equity, and inclusion—all reasonable requests. And yet, in a culture where only 25 percent of C-suite executives are women, most felt those requests were not being honored.[8] For every woman at the director level who gets a promotion, two women directors are voluntarily leaving their organizations.[9] Something's gotta give.

Of course, it's not just women leaders who suffer from systemic prejudice. Leaders of color of all genders often fare even worse. A recent study funded by Disney, Pfizer, and other major players in the corporate world revealed that Black professionals occupy only 3.2 percent of the senior leadership roles at large companies in the United States—and just 0.8 percent of all Fortune 500 CEO positions.[10]

Marginalized leaders are far more likely to encounter bias in the workplace. More than half of women report subtle, indirect forms of discrimination, both verbal and nonverbal. They get interrupted, mistaken for someone more junior, questioned in their area of expertise, denied credit for their contributions, or passed over for promotions.[11] These phenomena are called microaggressions—statements, actions, or incidents regarded as an instance of indirect, subtle, or unintentional discrimination against members of a marginalized group. Microaggressions can happen to men, too, of course, but women leaders were up to three times more likely to experience microaggressions than their male colleagues.

Often these microaggressions are unintentional. They're sparked by unconscious bias and other systemic problems; many people are truly unaware their behavior is causing harm. But because so many of us worry we may face backlash or serious repercussions, we don't speak out about what's happening. An *Harvard Business Review* study on racial discrimination in the workplace found that only 29 percent of Black professionals who experienced microaggressions reported them.[12]

These studies—and many others—are proof that the system is broken. It's time for a change. And as challenging as it may be, that change needs to start with us. We need to understand and own our part in the architecture. We need to first take a clear-eyed look at ourselves.

It's easy to feel like we're already doing that. Many women leaders are "leaning in" and trying to "level up," only to find that we aren't being set up for success—nor are we setting ourselves up for success. That's because we are holding ourselves back and allowing ourselves to be mistreated by our supervisors, peers, and even our subordinates.

One of my big epiphanies came when I realized how unprepared I was for senior leadership roles, especially the CEO and board positions I stepped into. This lack of preparation had nothing to do with my intelligence, experience, talents, or abilities; it was more . . . psychological—and informational. I didn't realize how different and difficult these high-stakes, powerful environments operated because 1) I'd never been told, and 2) I hadn't been socialized to navigate those environments and excel in them. This meant my inner demons and shadows would emerge at the most inopportune times and produce more internal barriers on top of the existing external barriers. I had always seen the glass ceilings above me, but didn't realize I had a glass ceiling inside of me as well. In addition to not recognizing the hostility surrounding me, I also found myself getting in my own way.

Before you shine brightly for the outside world, you must see yourself clearly.

You Can Change Your Experience

I've mentored and supported many leaders who have been sidelined as they attempted to advance. I've also seen the insidious ways marginalized professionals face unique challenges when navigating leadership roles.

But we are not powerless to change our environments, either. There are tangible steps we can take, efficient strategies we can deploy to create the kinds of careers we desire and deserve. We can make the kind of impact that may have seemed like a pipe dream in the past. If we want to manifest external opportunities, we have to do the internal work first. Only then can we access the self-trust, support, and resources we need to thrive.

I spent many years living with fear, insecurity, doubt, and shame (FIDS), even as I became increasingly successful. Forging a new path has required tremendous psychological, emotional, and spiritual growth. I have confronted truths about myself I'd always known but conveniently buried. I've reflected on past work environments that both hurt and healed me. It's not the journey I would have chosen for myself, but it's the one I had to embark on to step into my power.

So what did I do with the lessons I learned?

I wrote them down.

As Sally Ride said, "You can't be what you can't see." We need mirrors—people who reflect back our true selves, our potential, and our brilliance when we cannot see it ourselves. These mirrors are not merely passive reflectors; they actively illuminate parts of us that remain in shadow, helping us recognize strengths we've overlooked and possibilities we've never imagined. In writing this book, I hope to be that mirror for you—to show you the leader you already are beneath layers of doubt and conditioning.

The Mirror Effect occurs when we surround ourselves with people who see us clearly and reflect our authentic power back to us. This reflection builds resilience against the distorted images others may project onto us and creates a foundation of self-trust that no external force can shake. I am living proof that the insights, strategies, and lessons in this book can—and will—transform your life. The key is to give yourself time to absorb and adopt them, and to realize not everyone will support you as you go. But the ones who do become your mirrors—the people who will accept and support you, lift you up, and reflect your brilliance throughout your journey.

Holding Up Your Own Mirror

While external mirrors—those supporters and allies who reflect your brilliance back to you—are essential on your leadership journey, perhaps the most powerful mirror of all is the one you hold up to yourself. Many of us have become so accustomed to seeing ourselves through others' distorted lenses that we've lost sight of our true capabilities and worth.

Self-reflection is equivalent to acknowledging our weaknesses, but it's much more than just that. It's about recognizing your unique strengths, talents, and the wisdom you've gained through your experiences. As women and other marginalized leaders, we've often internalized external criticisms and biases to the point where our inner voice sounds suspiciously like our harshest critics.

I've learned that holding up your own mirror means developing the courage to question those internalized narratives. When that voice says, "You don't belong here" or "You're not qualified enough," pause and ask yourself: Is this truly my voice? Or is it an echo of biases I've encountered throughout my career?

The practice of holding up your own mirror requires brutal honesty balanced with profound compassion. It means celebrating your victories without diminishment and examining your missteps with curiosity rather than shame. It's about seeing yourself clearly—not through the fog of societal expectations or the distortions of workplace bias.

When I began this practice, I started keeping a "validation file"—a collection of accomplishments, positive feedback, and moments when I knew without doubt that I had made a meaningful impact. On days when imposter syndrome threatens to overtake me, this file serves as my personal mirror, reflecting back evidence of my capabilities that no one can dispute.

Holding up your own mirror also means giving yourself permission to be a work in progress. None of us arrives fully formed in leadership positions. We learn, we grow, and yes, sometimes we stumble. The authentic mirror reflects both your present strengths and your potential for growth without judgment.

You need to know yourself, your triggers, and your tendencies so you can address them. You have to understand your environment to know if it's toxic or healthy, reading between the lines of what people are saying and *not* saying. And you must believe in yourself and your own power so you can step into the right role, in the right place, at the right time as your authentic best self.

If you can do the inner work we'll be exploring in this book, you will be able to see situations more clearly. You'll recognize the ways you are affected by internal and external circumstances, and you'll be empowered to confront the fear, doubt, and shame you've been conditioned to feel. There is no man behind the curtain, and there is nothing to fear. I now know that I absolutely belong in that room, and you should, too. But you've got to do the inner work to truly trust yourself.

Once you understand *why* you feel these things, you can begin to break old patterns and show up differently. All those times you've felt undervalued, questioned, challenged, or less than? You'll have a playbook for how to respond. And that's just the beginning.

Of course, it hasn't been all brilliant reflections and the best of intentions. I've had board members ask me, "Who do you think you are?" or tell me, "Sorry—I can't go to bat for you because I want to work with these investors again." I've had bosses whom I thought were my mentors tell me, "I know how to manipulate you. I can push all your buttons," or "You misunderstand the situation. We've already discussed this, and I'm not going to talk about it again." I've learned that there is a *different playbook* at the most senior levels of organizations where big decisions are made and billion-dollar fates are determined. Information that's often shared behind the doors of an overwhelmingly white and middle-aged or, just frankly, *old* boys' club and corporate brotherhood. But finding that out for myself took time and lessons learned the hard way.

When I started out in the C-suite, I didn't understand the rules of the game and the politics at play. To complicate matters, I had my own internal challenges, as many of us do. We may suffer from racial or generational trauma. We may be limited by self-doubt and internalized blame. We often find ourselves working twice as hard for half the credit, and when we inevitably fall short, our critical inner judges take the wheel. These internal struggles make it even more difficult to achieve what we want to achieve in our careers. We're not setting *ourselves* up for success.

When you walk into a boardroom and you're the only woman—or the only woman of color—or the only queer person—or the only person with a disability—you're not seen or heard in the same manner as those around you. You are automatically at a disadvantage. Unfortunately, we've grown up in these unsafe environments all our lives. Many of us have become comfortable being uncomfortable.

To be clear, I'm not referring to the productive discomfort that comes with growth—pushing beyond our comfort zones to learn new skills or tackle challenges. Rather, I'm talking about the harmful discomfort that comes from persistent disenfranchisement: enduring microaggressions, being routinely overlooked for opportunities, having our ideas dismissed, being sexualized or objectified, and facing countless other subtle and not-so-subtle forms of discrimination. We've normalized these experiences to survive in environments that weren't designed for us, accepting a baseline of discomfort as simply "the way things are." This accommodation to chronic discomfort doesn't serve us—it depletes our energy, undermines our ability to trust ourselves, and limits our potential.

For so many years, I didn't understand the reality of some of these situations, nor was I equipped to deal with them. Often the only one like me in the room, I was saddled with self-limiting beliefs, biases, and conditioning.

But I no longer feel alone and helpless. And I don't want you or anyone else to feel that way, either. It's the reason why I decided to write this book and share my hard-learned lessons—to be a mirror for others who may be struggling to see their brilliance and potential shining back at them.

In 2021, emerging out of the COVID pandemic and after years of watching women leaders—including me—be sidelined, undermined, and undervalued in the biotech space, I decided to create something different. I called a friend and said, "Let's finally do this. Let's get a group of women

CEOs together, including women of color. It's time to form a powerful alliance, support one another, and share our stories, because we need and deserve a network of support."

Along with two brilliant female biotech chief executive officers, I helped to found a group of exceptional women leaders. What started as a small group of women at our first annual summit has now expanded to include more than two hundred members, all female biotech CEOs. We call ourselves the Biotech CEO Sisterhood.[13] Our focus is on mentorship and networking opportunities, lifting each other up and supporting one another in myriad ways, helping each other build our teams and companies. We work to find excellent board members, connect and reference investors, and form new ventures together, among many other imperatives. We are each other's mirrors.

The Biotech CEO Sisterhood has been one of the most meaningful initiatives in my life. I've never been part of such a supportive group of women. Not since my first CEO role, or maybe even before that—when I was serving as CMO and medical director at some of the world's biggest biotech and pharmaceutical companies. Or perhaps even earlier, sometime before med school ended, when I was falling in love with immunology in a dark lab somewhere in the icy depths of a Chicago winter. Together we are forging a vision to transform our industry.

And why stop with one industry when we have the power to change them all?

In this book, I will share the lessons we've taught and learned from each other. I'll share our stories so you can draw inspiration from them to stand strong in the face of adversity and be true to yourself.

I also invite our colleagues and leaders who are not disenfranchised to read this book and go on this journey with us, including white men. You are officially invited to be an honorary member of the Sisterhood regardless of your gender or identity markers. We need your support as allies if we are going to make a difference. We have all worked with men who are active supporters of women and have championed some of the most powerful women leaders today. They are invested in changing the system and want to make a better world for their daughters, wives, sisters, mothers, and *all* girls and women.

Step into Your Power

If you can absorb and adopt the lessons in this book, you'll be able to:

- Listen to your body and tune in to your authentic self to identify the internal factors that hold you back from achieving your biggest goals
- Let go of the behavioral patterns that don't serve you
- Recognize, evaluate, and move through (or out of!) hostile environments
- Step into high-powered positions without doubting your unique genius
- Treasure your authenticity without worrying what other people think
- Find a work environment worthy of your greatness
- Build a board of brilliant, talented, and experienced mirrors who are invested in your success
- Master complex conversations and negotiate with ease
- Own your own energy and refuse to take anyone else's bullshit
- Lead with empathy and strength, compassion and courage

My goal is to help you cultivate the awareness and strength as a leader to walk away from toxic situations toward something better. And you *can* do it. I've seen so many gifted leaders like Sara create an entirely different experience for themselves—and an empowering new life.

You deserve freedom from the limiting beliefs you've lugged around from job to job, relationship to relationship. You deserve to surround yourself with a potent and enthusiastic network of supporters to mirror your achievements and opportunities. I want to empower you to face the fear and insecurity, the doubt and searing shame. When you confront the parts of yourself you've always kept in the shadows, you illuminate the path forward.

But to do that, we must first go deep.

CHAPTER 2

HOW TO BECOME UNSHAKABLE

Naming Fear, Insecurity, Doubt, and Shame

"If you take care of your mind, you take care of the world."

–Arianna Huffington

What's your inner voice saying to you right now?

You know the one I mean. The one that sits deep inside, ready to critique you, judge you, put you in your place. Some call it your inner critic, but it's more complex. The voice isn't just yours; it comprises everyone who has ever berated or belittled you. Listen closely and you can hear the echoes of parents who were never satisfied, bosses who said you weren't good enough, colleagues and classmates whispering in your ear that you do not belong, in direct and indirect ways.

My friend, a clarity catalyst coach, calls this voice the "itty bitty shitty committee." And if that description sounds familiar, it's not just you.

People from underrepresented groups face more challenges, both internally and externally, than our majority peers. We grapple with external issues such as conditioning, racism, misogyny, and historical and cultural trauma. According to the Center for Law and Social Policy, historical trauma refers to profound collective suffering that affects generations of people united by shared identity or circumstances. The related concept of cultural trauma occurs when a group experiences devastating events that permanently alter their collective consciousness and fundamentally transform how they understand themselves moving forward. Shouldering historical trauma creates more obstacles for us—mentally and physically. The effects are pervasive and long-lasting. Studies have shown that they can affect physical and behavioral health and have been associated with addiction, higher rates of suicide, and cardiovascular disease.[1]

We bear the weight of complicated histories. Those histories have led to deep-seated fear, doubt, and shame. We are often unaware of the ways in which they drive us to succeed in our careers and lives—and the ways in which they hold us back.

Anyone can feel afraid. Any leader may feel like an imposter. We've all experienced doubt—even the white men in that boardroom. Of course, they have; that's just part of being human. But disenfranchised leaders often feel these things more pointedly because of our conditioning. We don't have the confidence and sense of safety other leaders take for granted because we've never felt like we belonged. So, we do our best to compensate.

We ignore the discomfort blooming in our chests when someone says or does something to us that we know is wrong. We overextend ourselves. We try to keep everyone happy and micromanage our presence, our tasks, and our teams so we don't mess up, all while we lock our authentic selves away where they won't cause trouble. The more we compromise our authenticity, the more isolated we feel.

But we *do* belong. We *do* deserve a seat at the table. In the words of the late, great Ruth Bader Ginsburg, "Women belong in all places where decisions are being made. It shouldn't be that women are the exception." That extends to everyone who doesn't look or sound or feel like the majority.

And yet, getting to those places comes at a cost. The tactics and behaviors we use to climb the ladder may not serve us when we finally reach the upper echelons of organizations. People-pleasing, taking on others' work, being obsequious to those in power—these strategies may have helped us advance, but they don't help us succeed in the long run.

This means we must up our game. We can harness tools to face our external and internal obstacles and begin to level the playing field so that *all* of us can walk into a room with the same knowledge, skills, and support networks as our colleagues have enjoyed their whole careers.

The first step is awareness. We must realize what we're feeling to identify the events, situations, and experiences that trigger us—eliciting strong emotional responses like fear, shame, or doubt. We must become our own mirrors. We will all face them, whether they arise from being gaslit, manipulated, bullied, or simply underestimated. But once we generate more self-awareness, we can understand *why* we're feeling fear and doubt and learn to address them proactively. **We can feel calm, centered, and connected to our authentic selves—for the benefit of ourselves, our businesses, and our communities.**

> **We can feel calm, centered, and connected to our authentic selves—for the benefit of ourselves, our businesses, and our communities.**

Throughout my career, I've been desperately afraid of not living up to the expectations other people set for me and the ones I set for myself. Not just as an executive, but as a wife and mom. I've been plagued by insecurity, often resorting to people-pleasing to try and prove my worth. I have sat with fear and doubt, and I am intimately acquainted with the feeling that fuels them: shame.

For most of my life, I assumed I was the cause of these feelings. In a way, I was right. I hadn't done the inner work to interrogate *why* I felt these things or where they came from. I didn't see shame for what it truly was: a hugely limiting belief doing its darndest to hold me back.

But there were also forces outside my control shaping me into a fearful, insecure, doubting, shame-filled person. I couldn't see the conditioning that began when I was a child, the biases I carried around about myself and other people. And since I had no awareness of the deeply flawed system I was trying to navigate, I thought I was the problem every time.

It wasn't just me, of course. There was an entire community of disenfranchised people who were silently suffering right there beside me, even though none of us said a word.

It took decades to realize that I was being triggered in the first place and to identify the causes of those triggers—generational and experiential. When I did, it changed everything for me. Please know that I don't use the word "trigger" lightly. Instead, I want to acknowledge the true weight of my experiences—and those of other historically marginalized people—and what can come up for us in interactions at work and beyond. I want to talk openly about the response patterns so many of us face. I want to speak from my own experience of what I now call "FIDS"—**fear, insecurity, doubt, and shame**—because I want us all to become **unshakable**. When we break our silence, we tap into our collective power to change the game.

What do I mean when I say unshakable? I don't mean that you'll never feel triggered by difficult situations—as humans, that's impossible. We're wired to react. What I do mean is developing the ability to remain steady and composed even when faced with challenges that would typically throw you off-balance. You can reduce your reactive tendencies so they're less easily provoked, and you can catch yourself early in the reaction process—before the train leaves the station, so to speak. (Keep in mind, too, that I am not a psychologist. I don't even play one on TV. While I offer advice about how to address triggers and reactions here, it's always a good idea to work with a professional to address trauma and corresponding challenges, past and present.)

Late coach and leadership embodiment expert Wendy Palmer, who is also a seventh-degree Aikido Black Belt, applied martial arts principles to her leadership teachings. She taught us that becoming unshakable is about working with both our bodies and minds. "The body always wins," she would often tell my coach, who was a student of hers. When we work with our bodies first, the rest of us can follow.

It's not your fault you're reacting. You've been conditioned to accept certain behaviors, languages, expectations, and cultural norms since you were a child. Our entire culture tells you how you are supposed to respond in certain situations: Sit down and shut up. Be grateful. Keep the peace. Subjugate your own needs to gratify someone else's. Stop complaining. Work harder. Don't mess up. Smile. Laugh.

The messages we're given on a daily basis—whether by bosses, colleagues, parents, spouses, or anyone who'd like us to cleave to their expectations—can be upsetting. Even when we're taught to accommodate them by any means necessary. **But the more deeply you know yourself and your own values, the better equipped you'll be to walk away unscathed.**

> **But the more deeply you know yourself and your own values, the better equipped you'll be to walk away unscathed.**

You can overcome fear of other people's opinions, or "FOPO," a term Dr. Michael Gervais coined to describe what he considered to be one of the greatest limiting factors on human potential. As he explains in his book, *The First Rule of Mastery*, "the key to leading a high-performance life is to redirect our attention from the world outside us to the world inside us."[2] I couldn't agree more. We need to identify and release our hidden barriers to step forward into our power and potential.

The only way to channel the dark currents into deeper self-knowledge is to confront them head-on, pouring light into the shadows. It's time to do the work.

The Hidden Cost of Fear, Insecurity, and Doubt

Feeling fear in the workplace is nothing new, especially for women. As a former biotech scientist and woman of color in STEM, Dr. Monica Mo, founder and CEO of WellSeek, has experienced gender bias, competitive gatekeeping, and sexual harassment. Drawing from her own experiences and those of other women in senior roles, she was inspired to conduct a larger study on all that we're up against.

"Nearly half of women fear taking personal time away from work," Dr. Mo wrote in an article for *Forbes*, "yet don't feel safe in the workplace. Caught in a matrix of external (social, family, career) and internal pressures, women are paying the price of the emotional toll and facing the brunt of the mental health crisis."[3]

As every woman knows, **we are conditioned from an early age to believe we're doing something—or even everything—wrong.** Girls are criticized for the way they dress. Moms are criticized for the way they parent. Senior executives are criticized for the way they lead. No wonder we walk around on eggshells, never knowing who will come after us next, or for what. We come to believe that if we're perfect, or as close to perfect as possible, we'll be safe from all that criticism. So we barricade ourselves into perceived safety with coping behaviors, only to find ourselves in a prison of our own creation. That prison of perfectionism has real consequences for our careers and our lives. As Tricia Montalvo Timm writes in *Chief*, "The tendency holds us back in several key ways. It discourages women from pursuing stretch assignments, applying for a new job, or asking for a raise until we're absolutely assured of success. Simultaneously, perfectionism is a major culprit when it comes to burnout since it drives us to take on too many tasks at work and at home."[4]

> **We are conditioned from an early age to believe we're doing something—or even everything—wrong.**

It can also wreak havoc on our personal lives. I have a brilliant friend who went to the most prestigious schools and worked at the best organizations in the world. But she had a deep fear of abandonment rooted in her childhood when she was separated from her mother for a long period of time. As a high-powered executive, she threw herself into her professional life—she was what we'd call a "workaholic"—and used her job to numb the pain of her one-way relationship with a man who didn't love or respect her. She had unwittingly recreated her childhood circumstances. When he ended things, she was devastated.

My friend tried to explain herself, analyzing how *she* was at fault for the breakup. Through deep, intensive therapy, she was able to grow to love and accept herself. She started her own company and now lives life on her terms. But it was a long road to get there. Until she identified the underlying fear dictating every decision she made, she couldn't heal.

I've felt afraid many times in my life, starting back when I was a little girl who wanted desperately to fit in but was ostracized by other kids because—in my predominantly white, rural town—I looked different. People from marginalized groups are particularly vulnerable to a fear of failure. Because we didn't fit into our neighborhoods growing up, our desire to belong caused us to develop coping mechanisms that stifle our true selves.

It's not like men, white people, and others in positions of power are never afraid. Fear of failure affects people of all sexes, genders, orientations, races, and nationalities. But for those of us who've been disenfranchised, it's more pronounced. It amplifies all the other fears playing in our heads: *If I fail, I won't be loved; I won't belong; I'll be nothing.* The implications feel destabilizing and potentially devastating. Failure makes us feel like we will disappear; that we'll become truly invisible. If we fail, will we get a second chance? Or is this it? We're balanced on a razor's edge, convinced we only get so many shots at the goal.

Many of us also feel extreme pressure to be the model minority. In a *Forbes* article on the pressure Black women feel to succeed, Candice Cook Simmons shared her insight as a C-suite executive and founder of the Cook Law Group. "As a double minority, Black women tend to have the added stress of taking on the responsibility to not only refute any myths or stereotypes surrounding women in the workplace by going far above just 'outstanding' work, but also setting new standards and reinforcing for others experiences of heightened levels of 'excellence' as it relates to people of color."[5]

Many of us channel our ambition into securing high-powered positions, hoping we will finally be accepted and appreciated. But even when we get them, we find we're not really welcome there. We'll never be good enough on our own merits; we need to put our heads down and defer to the people in power. This matches up with everything we've been conditioned to believe, so we work ourselves to the bone, trying desperately to prove our worth.

Unfortunately, the harder we try to prove our worth in a system designed to challenge and diminish it, the more the gap widens between the polished selves we present to others and the wild uncertainty we feel inside.

That uncertainty translates into insecurity. We find ourselves questioning our worth and abilities, growing surer by the day that we're not enough. Worse, we're sure everyone can see all the ways we fall short. As a result, we may feel anxious or uncomfortable in social situations, expecting judgment or rejection at every turn. That may make it hard to trust our teams, our boards, or even our friends.

> **Doubt is the voice in your head that says you're not good enough; that no matter how successful you are, you don't really deserve it.**

If fear and insecurity are what you feel when you're afraid of what's coming, doubt is when you second-guess yourself in the here and now. **Doubt is the voice in your head that says you're not good enough; that no matter how successful you are, you don't really deserve it.**

Maybe you've been a high achiever in your career. People admire you and depend on your expertise. What they don't know is that you constantly doubt yourself. That it eats away at you. You can make a lasting impact on thousands of people, amass a stack of accomplishments a mile high—and still feel you're not good enough.

Ellen Taaffe, a professor and director of women's leadership programs at the Kellogg School of Management, has observed how self-doubt can be particularly acute for high achievers.[6] Despite our experience and expertise, many of us can't shake the nagging feeling we aren't ready to step into high-powered roles and promotions. We are also more prone to perfectionism, which can make it difficult to act without 100 percent certainty. We may hold back in meetings, unsure that our contribution is valid or that it will garner enthusiastic support.

Or we may compensate for self-doubt by cranking up the charisma. We find ourselves putting up a façade, striving tirelessly to make it look like we have it all together. But the inner turmoil we feel—the gap between our external success and our internal doubt—is eating us from the inside out. And we can't talk to anyone about what we're feeling because we're already struggling with imposter syndrome. We walk around constantly afraid someone will expose us as the frauds we are, even when we're making a huge impact on our companies and communities.

Women of Influence+, a global organization committed to advancing gender equity in the workplace, released the results of an international research project called The Tallest Poppy study. Tall Poppy Syndrome occurs when women who have achieved great professional success—perhaps even towering above others in their field—are attacked, criticized, belittled, or cut down. Out of thousands of women from a wide variety of demographics and professions in 103 countries, a staggering 87 percent had experienced Tall Poppy Syndrome. Seventy-two percent reported being left out of important meetings; 71 percent said they were undermined because of their success; 68 percent had seen their achievements dismissed; 66 percent said others had taken credit for their work.[7] If we extrapolate from those numbers, we can assume that the majority of working women know exactly how it feels to be punished for taking up so much space.

Sometimes we're told outright that we don't deserve our roles or positions. People of color are still facing quiet backlash. White male authors have complained publicly that white men are having trouble getting writing jobs as victims of "reverse racism." Activists have brought multiple lawsuits against prestigious universities to challenge the legality of affirmative action policies, policies put in place to combat historic racial discrimination. Actors of color are told they are "diversity hires" in film and TV.

I know the feeling. As a woman of color, I've had plenty of people insinuate—or say outright—that I was only there to fill a quota. When I was accepted to MIT, that's exactly what I was told by my fellow high school students, even though my grades and scores were higher than theirs. Years later, after proving myself in numerous ways—as a physician, a drug developer, a leader, and more—I was told by a board member of my own company, "If I knew you were going to be CEO, I would have never joined this board." These are just a couple of examples of the many, many times I was dismissed, insulted, shamed, interrogated, and cut down to size by my peers, regardless of my accomplishments.

To manage the fear, insecurity, and doubt so many of us experience from these deeply ingrained biases, we might overcompensate, assuming everything is our fault, and we have to fix every problem—even the ones that don't belong to us. We might disengage from people at work, pouring all our energy into putting our heads down and working harder than everyone else. We might quit our jobs because we're so afraid of being rejected, believing it's better to reject ourselves before anyone else gets a chance. We might even hop from job to job, chasing that elusive validation.

There's no specific individual instruction manual for dismantling self-doubt and insecurity—or if there is, I haven't found it. I can't offer you a magical elixir to eradicate these feelings once and for all. However, I will tell you that you can heal yourself and find your authentic self.

If we want to become less agitated by our surroundings, we have to start with ourselves. Once we can identify what—and who—is upsetting us, we can begin the work of extricating our self-worth from the messages we're being given, both in words and in actions. We can face down our imposter syndrome from a stronger, more empowered place.

Shrink the Button: Defusing Your Triggers

Have you ever noticed how certain words or actions from others can instantly set you off? Perhaps someone questions your expertise in a meeting, speaks over you, or dismisses your ideas. That immediate emotional reaction—the surge of anger, shame, or defensiveness—is what I call your "button." For many of us, especially those from underrepresented groups, the feeling of being disrespected is one of our biggest buttons.

The good news? You can shrink that button until it's so small that no one can press it anymore.

Understanding Your Disrespect Button

At the core of many triggers is our fear of being disrespected or under-valued. When someone questions our expertise or talks over us, that button gets pressed, and we react—sometimes in ways that don't serve our best interests.

The key insight that transformed my own relationship with triggers was realizing this fundamental truth: **When I fully respect myself, I no longer need external validation to feel worthy.** This self-respect becomes an unshakable foundation that no external force can disturb.

When you access that rich resource of self-trust and respect within you, the power of others to trigger you diminishes dramatically. You're no longer dependent on someone else's validation to know your worth. This internal shift grants you tremendous freedom—freedom in your language, your boldness, your authenticity. You become more real, more juicy, more powerful.

Let's work through a practical exercise to help you shrink your own buttons:

1. **Identify Your Button:** Think about the last three times you felt triggered in a professional setting. Write down what happened, who was involved, and most importantly, what you believe the interaction said about you that caused such a strong reaction.

2. **Locate the Fear:** For each triggering situation, ask yourself: "What was I afraid was true about me in that moment?" Perhaps you feared being exposed as incompetent, or worried others would see you as unworthy of your position.

3. **Challenge the Fear:** Now, write evidence that contradicts each fear. List your qualifications, achievements, and

strengths that prove your capabilities. Remember times when you've excelled despite doubts.

4. **Create Your Self-Respect Mantra:** Based on your evidence, craft a short, powerful statement of self-validation that you can recall when triggered. For example: "I am extensively qualified, with unique insights that have repeatedly proven valuable."

5. **Practice Self-Validation:** The next time you feel that button being pressed, pause. Take a deep breath. Silently repeat your mantra to yourself. Notice how accessing your own self-respect changes your emotional response.

6. **Track Your Progress:** Note triggering incidents and how you responded. Over time, you'll likely notice that the same situations that once sent you into a tailspin now barely register as irritations.

Remember, becoming unshakable isn't about never feeling triggered—it's about developing such a strong foundation of self-respect that external validation becomes unnecessary. When you truly know your worth, others' opinions hold less power over your emotional state.

The more you practice this, the more you'll notice a profound shift: Your reactions become choices rather than automatic responses. You'll find yourself speaking more freely, showing up more authentically, and leading with greater confidence—not because others respect you more, but because you've fully claimed your own self-respect.

The Soul-Sucking Impact of Shame

Of course, it's not as easy as incorporating one simple exercise—or even many of them. Maybe you have done a lot of inner work like I had done for years without making much progress. You thought you had high emotional intelligence yet, you were blindsided again and again. This may be because there's another feeling gnawing at you, this one even darker than the rest. It's tangled up in fear, insecurity, doubt—and it's often the hardest one to shift: shame.

Much has been written about shame. Shame is the toxic underpinning of fear, insecurity, and doubt. It thrives on feelings of unworthiness and inferiority, making you feel disappointed not just in what you've accomplished, but in who you are. You may believe you're a bad person who doesn't deserve good things. Even on your most triumphant day, shame can sneak into your mind and heart, souring your joy.

Shame is the black hole that sucks up our energy and undermines self-trust. It is the invisible weight sitting in our chests, especially those of us who've faced personal, professional, and generational trauma. For marginalized leaders, shame can be a double whammy: Even when we are the ones who are wronged, we feel shame about it. A lifetime of conditioning has made us quick to assume something is wrong with *us*. This exacerbates the fear we have always carried inside that we won't be fully accepted. **We try so hard to prove ourselves, but deep down we feel a searing sense of shame that we will never be good enough.**

Brené Brown, author of *Daring Greatly,* says it best: "I don't believe shame is helpful or productive. In fact, I think shame is more likely to be the source of destructive, hurtful behavior than the solution or cure. Shame corrodes the very part of us that believes we are capable of change."[8]

I'm not a psychologist, but as a clinician and scientist I am interested in causality. Experts have identified several root causes of shame. It is often instilled in early childhood by parents or other authority figures who demean or diminish their kids.[9] It feeds on abandonment and rejection. Shame can be a result of verbal, physical, mental, or sexual abuse, and the resulting trauma that survivors experience. Poverty or chronic illness can plant the seeds of shame, which are then watered when a teenager or adult makes dangerous or harmful choices.

You'll notice considerable overlap between shame and people-pleasing. Those struggling with shame are often natural people-pleasers, trying to fill the holes they feel by making others happy.

Shame is like a weed: If it's not addressed, it spreads. If it's alive and well in one area of your life, it's more than happy to sprawl into another.

> **When we're busy shaming ourselves, it can feel next to impossible to take a step back and recognize what's happening. But it *is* possible.**

Let's say you're a senior executive who makes a mistake at work. It's not a big deal, but you feel ashamed that someone with your experience could make such an oversight. You can't stop thinking about it on the drive home. You replay the moment with your boss over and over, embarrassed by how you fell all over yourself to grovel and apologize.

The first thing your spouse says when you walk in the door is, "I thought you were picking up dinner." A fresh wave of shame washes over you. You *were* supposed to pick up dinner. How could you forget? Now your spouse is annoyed, and your kids are hungry. You've been so overwhelmed at work you haven't even had time to go grocery shopping. *Great. Now you're failing as a mother, too.*

These thought patterns can send us spiraling straight into imposter syndrome. You may be a high-powered executive, but clearly, you're an imposter who doesn't deserve the role. Everyone says you're a great mom, but they're obviously wrong about that, too. All your accolades mean nothing; you're convinced you faked your way into them. If anyone could see who you *really* are, all the ways you fail people on a daily basis, they'd strip it all away from you.

When we're busy shaming ourselves, it can feel next to impossible to take a step back and recognize what's happening. But it *is* possible. You first have to acknowledge that it *is* shame you're feeling. Not annoyance, embarrassment, or insecurity; not any of the less pernicious names we use to minimize the feeling. You have to name your shame.

Once you've named it—acknowledged that you've been shaken, and the feeling that's coming up for you is shame—then you can begin to dissect it. Where is the shame coming from? Is it possible these feelings have a history that began long before you forgot to pick up dinner or messed up at work? We have all been handed down a damaging belief system that has existed for centuries; it's part of our unconscious. If we could dismantle those beliefs and the shame they often carry, we'd live far richer, happier lives.

So how do we rewrite the narrative? We have to confront our thoughts, beliefs, and actions. For many of us this means learning an entirely new skill set than the one we've been taught and spent our whole life developing. To beat shame, we must first get honest with ourselves. Our *true* selves, the ones that have been crushed under years of fear, doubt, and shame. Then we must stand up, raise our voices, and tell the truth.

The Truth Will Set You Free

I have a dear friend with loads of talent and smarts. She was one of the top economic reporters in the country. Her commentary was brilliant; her analyses spot-on. The only problem was that people repeatedly told her she only got the job based on her looks, not her ability, and she internalized that narrative. My friend constantly put herself down, claiming she wasn't all that smart. Once she confessed to me that what she felt deep down was shame. She was convinced people only valued her for her beauty and was ashamed she didn't have the brains to back it up.

The truth—which I could see clearly, even if she couldn't—was that she *did* have the brains. She was far smarter than most of her colleagues! I could see the chain of events: Ever since she was a little girl, she was conditioned to believe her worth boiled down to the way she looked. That limiting belief was reinforced during young adulthood. "You're so pretty," she was told, over and over, until she came to believe her prettiness was her only value.

Once she became an adult, the world seemed to turn it against her, demeaning her for being "just a pretty face." She couldn't possibly have *earned* her successes, they said, due to her talent or drive. In a society where beauty is currency, she believed them.

As a result, this gifted, talented woman found herself stuck in what author and psychologist Tara Brach calls "the trance of unworthiness."[10] But she was able to break free.

It didn't happen overnight. Over a period of several years, with a lot of brave self-exploration and the help of a great therapist, she was able to cast off her shame.

It took her a while to acknowledge all the abuse she had suffered in her career, including repeated sexual harassment that had contributed to that deep sense of shame. That led to an epiphany: she didn't want to work for anyone anymore. Instead, she became an independent financial advisor.

My friend flourished in this new role. She wrote a book, appeared on multiple TV networks, and is now considered an expert in her field. And her success didn't stop there. She also started her own investment fund, building a team who studied the state of the markets and netted incredible returns.

All this happened because she let go of shame. Once she did that, she shed the self-doubt and imposter syndrome she had worn like a second skin for so long. She was able to identify the people and situations that negatively affected her, liberate herself from toxic environments, and create the kind of life she'd always wanted. I loved seeing her thrive. She was a rock star, which I'd always known—and finally, she believed it.

Navigate Shame

What do you do when you're in the midst of navigating shame?

Our bodies often signal that we're getting knocked off balance before our conscious minds register it. You might notice a sudden heat rising in your chest, a contraction in your stomach, or tension in your shoulders. These physical sensations are early warning signs—and catching them gives you a crucial window of opportunity to regain your composure before these reactions gain momentum.

When you notice these physical signs, try this centering practice: Take your attention off what's disturbing you and place it on your breath. Intentionally slow and extend your breathing, which activates your parasympathetic nervous system—your body's natural calming mechanism. When you feel threatened or challenged, you instinctively contract. Instead, consciously do the opposite: open, expand, and elongate your posture. This physical shift can create an energetic change that not only helps you maintain your equilibrium but also changes how others perceive and respond to you.

Another option comes from Catalyst, a nonprofit comprising multinational corporations and powerful leaders that is committed to building "workplaces that work for women."[11] Catalyst offers numerous courses to build a more equitable working world. One of the exercises they created to navigate shame has stuck with me:

1. **Name what's causing you shame.** Take some time to identify and clearly define the specific thoughts, actions, or situations that are causing you to feel shame. Write them down or speak them aloud to actively acknowledge and confront these feelings.

2. **Realize it's not true.** Challenge the validity of your shame-inducing beliefs. Understand that feelings of shame often stem from distorted or negative self-perceptions, many of which we've been socially conditioned to believe. Ask yourself questions like, "Is this belief based on facts and evidence?" or "Am I being overly critical of myself?" Realize, too, that your self-worth is not defined solely by your thoughts. We're so much more than we think!

3. **Bring in counterexamples.** Gather evidence and examples that contradict those shame-inducing beliefs. Think of

times when you've succeeded, received positive feedback, or acted in ways that directly contradict those beliefs. This step helps you see yourself in a more balanced and accurate way.

4. **Love yourself.** Practice self-compassion and self-acceptance. Treat yourself with the same kindness and understanding that you would offer to a friend, sibling, or child in a similar situation. I often try to treat myself as I would my daughter, cultivating a positive and nurturing inner dialogue, offering compassion for my humanity and any missteps or moments of imperfection that come with it.

By encouraging self-awareness, self-compassion, and a shift in perspective, this exercise serves as a powerful tool for addressing and mitigating feelings of shame. The results aren't instant—overcoming shame takes time and patience. After all, many of us have been grappling with these feelings for the majority of our lives. But the more you do this exercise—addressing and countering feelings of shame and practicing self-love—the more effective it will feel.

Expand Your Perspective

One powerful technique for maintaining your composure, especially in challenging conversations, is what I call "crossing the table." Physically imagine yourself getting up, walking around, and sitting in the chair next to the person opposite you. From there, temporarily take in their full perspective.

The key word here is *temporarily.* Many of us fear that if we step off our position at all, we're giving ground permanently. This is just a momentary move to gather information. Once you've seen the other person's full view, you can return to your position with new insights.

This practice, once you've settled your nervous system and returned to a centered state, allows you to see other perspectives clearly—and ultimately increases your influence while keeping you grounded and unshakable.

Byron Katie, an author and speaker who teaches a method of self-inquiry she calls "The Work," suggests a similar approach. "Notice, name, and feel the emotion you were experiencing at the time. Find the reason you were upset."[12] That's the very first step. Once you name it, you can reframe it.

Step into Your Power

So often, we're lying to ourselves, creating and reinforcing myths about who we are. To bust those myths, we must:

- **Fight lies with truth.** What lies do you believe about yourself? Where do fear, doubt, and shame rear their ugly heads? Maybe these lies are things you've been told about your failures or shortcomings, and you can still hear the accusing person's voice in your head. If so, don't write down the lies—we don't want to give them more power. Instead, write the truth that sits on the other side of that lie. What is your unique genius?
- **Believe in yourself and your worth.** What are three of your best qualities that make you proud? Write them down right now—more if you're inspired. If you have trouble with this exercise, think of three positive words your friends and family members would use to describe you. This will train you to move away from constructing your identity around *what you do* and begin to see the inherent gifts of *who you are*.

- **Find your inner resilience.** Think of three occasions in your life when authority figures got a rise out of you. Times when you felt set on edge, or when you backed down, deferred to their perspective, and blamed yourself. This could be a childhood memory—perhaps an overbearing parent or teacher verbally or emotionally abusing you—or an incident at work where a boss berated or talked down to you in a public setting. Write down as many details as you can recall. Can you describe the physical sensations you felt? What negative messages did you take away?

  With the benefit of hindsight, rewrite each narrative with how you would respond today, now that you have greater awareness and better tools. Doing this exercise will teach you how to recognize similar situations when they arise in the future, setting you up for success.

If you'd like to deepen this work, *The Mirror Effect Workbook & Journal* provides structured exercises to help you identify and navigate your FIDS patterns. The daily prompts guide you through recognizing your triggers and developing compassionate responses to fear, insecurity, doubt, and shame, transforming how you respond to challenging situations. You can get yours at SheilaGujrathiMD.com.

I must also note that this is an excellent time to reach out to a therapist or trained coach. I would never have been able to go as deep into my inner work without the wisdom and guidance of a good therapist and several executive coaches throughout my career. My therapist helped me face my triggers, wade through painful past experiences, and know myself better. Similarly, my executive coaches provided invaluable perspective as I navigated the complex politics and challenges of rising through the ranks in large organizations and later running my own companies.

These professionals created a safe space where I could be vulnerable about my fears and doubts without judgment. They offered objective feedback when I couldn't see my own blind spots and helped me develop strategies to overcome the internal barriers that were holding me back. Perhaps most importantly, working with coaches and therapists made me feel less alone during some of the most challenging periods of my professional life. It's a profound relief to have someone in your corner who understands the unique pressures faced by leaders from historically marginalized backgrounds.

I highly recommend making this investment in yourself. The return on that investment—in terms of your self-awareness, emotional resilience, and leadership effectiveness—is immeasurable.

Note, too, that developing an unshakable presence requires self-compassion. While understanding the "why" behind our reactions has value, what matters most is recognizing when we're off-balance and regaining our stability. Show yourself generosity and kindness—your history and past conditioning have brought you to this point, but they don't define where you go from here.

Compassion, even more than confidence, is the foundation for becoming unshakable. And it always starts with the self. As you work with these techniques and encounter difficult individuals, extend that same compassion outward. This doesn't mean accepting bad behavior—it means approaching challenging situations from a centered, grounded place where you remain steady regardless of what comes your way.

Ultimately, you can uproot any fear, doubt, and shame you may be carrying around. The process is not always easy or fun. Sometimes I imagine the mythical phoenix, burning to ash so she can emerge stronger. You have to do the same. You must stare into the eyes of your demons, and confront the doubts and fears that have defined you up until now. If that means burning down what no longer serves you, I'll hand you the match.

CHAPTER 3

THE FOUR ARCHETYPES
Breaking Through the Inner Glass Ceiling

"There's always going to be somebody telling you you don't belong and you can't do this. You've got to practice a different set of tools."

–Michelle Obama

What archetypes are you playing in life and work—and how are they holding you back?

First introduced by Swiss psychoanalyst Carl Jung, the concept of archetypes originally referred to universal, inherited patterns in the collective unconscious of all human beings. Today the term is often co-opted by brands, corporations, and coaches to label people and sort them into recognizable groups.

Think of archetypes as the roles we play. They're personas we embody for a variety of reasons—familial, cultural, professional. Archetypes have a long lineage, and when we take them on, we inherit specific habits and behaviors that surface in all aspects of our lives.

At home you might be the Caregiver, the one who does the majority of the labor, whether it's logistical—like cooking or childcare—or the emotional labor of holding the family together. Maybe you identify more with the Martyr, prioritizing the well-being of your kids or partner, even if it means sacrificing your own needs.

At work you may habitually step into the role of the Hero, always ready to sweep in and save the day. Or you could be the Peacemaker, known by your colleagues as the one who quashes brewing conflict.

Archetypes aren't inherently bad; they can help you recognize highly valuable skill sets within yourself. Maybe you resonate with the Creator, the Problem-Solver, or the Sage, roles that bring you joy and fulfillment. The trouble comes when these personas prevent you from stepping into your true power and authenticity since they don't always allow for the full expression of who you are and the unique gifts you have to offer. Instead, they become an inner glass ceiling, a combination of self-limiting beliefs and FIDS that hold you back. This is especially true at work.

To be the best executives and leaders we can be, we have to be able to read the room and fulfill different archetypes at different times. When you understand the archetypes people tend to fall into at work, you can wield that knowledge to your advantage. You can show up powerfully and intentionally based on the situation to get the best possible outcome.

Getting to that place of flexibility requires us to first identify the prescribed roles we may be playing, either consciously or unconsciously. Then we can ask ourselves: Does this serve me or hold me back? Or is there another way I could be moving through the world and leading my company?

From my personal experience, as well as countless conversations I've had with other marginalized business leaders, I see four harmful types that surface most often: the **People-pleaser**, the **Imposter**, the **Bitch Boss**, and the **Micromanager**.

If any of these archetypes sound uncomfortably familiar, please don't blame yourself. You've adopted one or more of these personas to survive and succeed in your personal and professional life. They've helped you get by in one way or another, and that's important. But they've also forced you into a box, and you may have been in there so long, you don't even realize you're trapped. In so many ways, the roles we play both protect and limit us. And just as with FIDS, we need to talk about them. Only by digging into the tendencies that hold us back can we set ourselves free.

Stop Should-ing on Yourself

Archetypes tend to come with an implicit *should*. How you *should* act as a woman or person of color; how you *should* parent your kids; how you *should* lead a company. The workplace is particularly fertile ground for this kind of social conditioning, especially for those of us who've had to work twice as hard for half the credit. This constant *should*ing only makes us more easily affected—which ironically sends us running back to one (or more) of our archetypes as a coping mechanism.

But once you recognize the inner glass ceiling and its corresponding behaviors, you can notice and name them. Better yet, you can take the best of the archetypes and shatter the rest. When we're truly aware of how they show up in our lives, we can hold on to the parts that benefit us and let go of the components that don't—or deploy them situationally to make sure they're actually making our lives better.

Let's start with the People-pleaser, an archetype many of us know well—myself included.

The People-Pleaser

People-pleasers want everyone to like them. They're nice, non-confrontational, and usually averse to conflict. They are generally well-liked—and why wouldn't they be? They're pleasant to be around and habitually do what they're told.

People-pleasers also:

- Find it hard to refuse requests
- Overcommit to plans, responsibilities, or projects
- Don't advocate for their own needs
- Go along with things they aren't happy about to avoid friction[1]

Of course, people-pleasing comes at a price. According to *Psychology Today*, People-pleasers are "largely insecure. They want to be well-liked, feel needed, feel appreciated, and feel useful. They do not rely on independent thinking, and they lack the self-trust to do so. Often, they do not even recognize how they feel. If they don't please others, they worry about being disapproved of and dismissed."[2]

People-pleasers bend over backward to make other people like and respect them. At work, that often means they take on more than they should and sacrifice their personal lives—all for the sake of making other people happy.

Again, this isn't your fault. People-pleasing is deeply rooted in a need to survive. Friction and disapproval are terrifying when they can jeopardize your position or career. When I've succumbed to people-pleasing in past leadership roles, fear has always been at the core. Many of the leaders I've met feel the same way. We're desperate to avoid pushback from anyone. If it sparks a conflict, it might cause people to dislike us, and then what if we lose everything we've worked so hard to achieve?

How do People-pleasers respond to setbacks? They put their heads down and work even harder. Anything to keep people happy and not rock the boat. This is why many People-pleasers fall into the trap of "servant leadership," a term that's been popularized in recent years, especially by those in power. It sounds nice in theory; in practice, it can be deceptive. For marginalized leaders, being a servant leader often entails accepting blame for things that aren't our fault. That, too, is part of our social conditioning. We cling to the idea that if we do exactly what everyone wants and make sure no one's mad at us, we'll become full members of society.

Unfortunately, this behavior is directly at odds with the traits leaders need to succeed. Chronic People-pleasers can't make the kinds of hard decisions senior executives have to make—decisions that some people won't like. They haven't developed the skills for making tough calls, like canceling a project or firing a direct report. They agree to do tasks and errands they don't have time for and hire candidates who aren't right for the role. They treat their colleagues like friends and family, unable to see them as the employees they are.

And as a result, People-pleasers find themselves between a rock and a hard place. Despite their experience and expertise, they get passed over for promotions or told they "don't have what it takes." They are perpetually stuck in limbo, trying to please people to advance in their careers, when in fact their people-pleasing tendencies are keeping them stuck—bumping up against that inner glass ceiling time and again.

Since People-pleasers struggle to say no, they commonly feel stressed and overwhelmed, which can result in resentment and passive-aggressive behaviors. But they rarely complain or call out unfair treatment; they're too afraid of punishment or reprisal.

People-pleasers mistake a lack of overt conflict for a good outcome, but that's not the case. Making sure everyone around you is happy all the time simply isn't your job. And it doesn't mean you're making good decisions. Plus, if you're intent on making everyone happy (an impossible and time-consuming endeavor), you're most likely not doing your actual job.

More importantly, you're doing yourself a disservice. You can't be true to yourself when you're solely focused on pleasing others. If you seek constant validation and praise, it becomes impossible to develop your authentic leadership style. You keep subjugating your own wants and needs because they might conflict with someone else's. So you mold your personality around others—and surrender your power.

I want to make a distinction here between people-pleasing niceness and kindness. It is possible to be kind without being "nice." In fact, sometimes those two things are in direct conflict. An *Inc.* article on effective leadership urges leaders to "stop being nice and start being kind. Telling a flailing employee they're flailing with the aim of helping them improve isn't very nice. But it is kind. Calling out bias in a meeting isn't nice, it's awkward. It is also kind."[3]

Genuine kindness creates space for us to be our authentic selves. According to Project Happiness, a nonprofit studying the science of happiness: "While niceness maintains a facade that our lives are together and assumes that same status quo for others, kindness gives permission for real success and failure."[4]

Leading with kindness is a generous and valuable approach. It's also intentional. Leaders with a deep and sometimes neurotic need to please others act out of obligation. Their actions come from a place of fear, whether they know it or not.

Given all this, it's no surprise that People-pleasers are perfect targets for bullies and people in power. If you come across as overly eager to please and your colleagues know you'll do anything for their approval, you've essentially painted a target on your back. Remember all those board chairs named John from the *Fortune* study? They may take advantage of you. Not all of them, of course—I've worked with hundreds of men who are wonderful, supportive champions, and leaders who make space for marginalized voices to be heard. Others may simply ask you to do more without thinking much of it.

Though you may have logged fewer hours in leadership, you've probably been playing the people-pleasing game for a long time. This behavior is often instilled in us as children. People raised in authoritarian households by parents who punished them for making mistakes—or by "tiger parents" who pressured them to be high achievers—are far more susceptible to a pathological need to please.[5] Childhood trauma can be another factor. And if you saw people-pleasing modeled by your parents or other adults you looked up to, you may have unconsciously followed suit. Most archetypes have a long lineage, and people-pleasing is no different. It's the kind of self-limiting behavior no one wants to inherit, yet so many of us do.

So how do we escape from the people-pleasing trap?

The answer is simple: **Accept that you can't make everyone happy.** If you want to be a powerful leader, you must make decisions that are right for the company—and right for *you*—even when they're unpopular.

Simple doesn't mean easy. When you've spent your whole life as a People-pleaser, it becomes a reflex. That's why the first step is to **stop and notice**.

Habits can be especially hard to detect because most of us aren't even aware we have them. Start by listening for certain words you find yourself repeating. "Yes" is a huge one—especially when everything in you is telling you to say *no*. People-pleasers often say "sorry" when there's no need to apologize. When you hear yourself taking the blame or excusing some-

Accept that you can't make everyone happy.

one else's faults, pay attention. You might try tallying all those "yeses" and "sorries" in a note on your phone to see just how many you utter in a week. This is how we cultivate awareness: one word, one reaction at a time. Tune in to the moments when your mouth is saying words that don't align with your gut. And while you're at it: pay attention to who sets off this behavior in you, as well as what situations cause it. Write it all down —that's extremely helpful information to have.

Many People-pleasers are convinced others will think they're self-serving if they voice a genuine opinion or say, "No." But focusing on the needs of others at the cost of your own is not sustainable. Ultimately it's bad for you *and* the people you're trying to please; you're robbing them of your authentic leadership. So **don't fear being selfish**. Guess what truly selfish people *don't* worry about? Being selfish! They're too self-involved to care.

Another way to combat people-pleasing? **Connect with something deeper than yourself**. Faith, spirituality, source—whatever you want to call it, we all hold beliefs that bring meaning and purpose to our lives. Even those who don't identify as religious believe in something: science, the power of human kindness, the importance of environmental stewardship. When it comes to people-pleasing, it can be profoundly empowering to drop down deeper into ourselves, making space for that quiet, grounded voice of wisdom telling us that we are the only people we truly need to please.

As Gina DeVee, a women's empowerment mentor who's written about archetypes, says in her book *The Audacity to Be Queen*: "The cure for this toxic, paralyzing *disease to please* starts with getting your security from your spiritual connection instead of the peanut gallery. Time to give yourself permission to be the real you."[6]

But what if you're convinced the real you isn't good enough? What if you're not even sure who the real you *is*?

That brings us to archetype number two.

The Imposter

Before we dig into this type, I want to make an important distinction. The Imposter we're talking about is not *actually* an imposter. Rather, it's someone suffering from imposter *syndrome*.

Merriam-Webster's first definition of "syndrome" is the standard medical one: a group of signs and symptoms that characterize a particular condition. But the secondary definition is enlightening: "a set of concurrent things, such as emotions or actions, that usually form an identifiable pattern."[7] We've arrived back at the idea of patterns, internalized habits, and behaviors we keep bumping up against. It follows, then, that imposter syndrome is defined as a psychological condition "characterized by persistent doubt concerning one's abilities or accomplishments, accompanied by the fear of being exposed as a fraud—despite evidence of one's ongoing success."[8]

Despite evidence of one's ongoing success. Even the dictionary makes this distinction: having imposter syndrome is different from being an actual imposter. The people who exhibit symptoms of imposter syndrome are typically flourishing. They are successful professionals, exceptional parents, loyal friends—and yet they themselves can't see it. They perpetually feel like frauds and outsiders. They're convinced that no matter how successful they are or how much they've accomplished, they don't really deserve it. According to *Psychology Today*, people with imposter syndrome "often attribute their accomplishments to external or transient causes such as luck, good timing, or effort that they cannot regularly expend."[9]

But even considering it a "syndrome" is a gaslighting of sorts, since these fears about being imposters are actually externally derived. Ruchika Tulshyan and Jodi-Ann Burey, two incisive thought leaders and women of color, published an article in *Harvard Business Review* peeling back the layers of imposter syndrome to diagnose what's really going on. "For many women," they write, "feeling like an outsider isn't an illusion. It's the result of systemic bias and exclusion."[10] Imposter syndrome doesn't stem from some character flaw or personal failing. The system tells us we are Imposters our whole lives until, finally, we believe it.

Imposter archetypes often find themselves thinking:

- "It's only a matter of time before everyone realizes I'm a fraud."
- "People are only being nice to me because they feel obligated to."
- "I don't deserve this position."
- "Should I even be here?"

Even if you can point to specific achievements and a proven track record of success, you never feel good enough. You play out scenarios for how to back out of the limelight into a more comfortable position where you won't be exposed. You judge yourself and your accomplishments, engaging in negative self-talk about everything you *haven't* done. Your mind is skilled at psychological aerobics: it can flip your greatest triumph into your darkest failure.

So where does imposter syndrome come from?

Interestingly, this archetype can evolve under similar conditions as the People-pleaser. As a child, the Imposter may have had hypercritical parents or an overbearing authority figure—a coach, a teacher—who made them feel like no matter what they did, they were missing the mark.

Maybe they were compared unfavorably to their siblings, mistreated, or devalued in the family hierarchy. If they survived trauma, they might struggle with self-worth, certain they didn't deserve their own success.

Studies have revealed other contributing factors that may lead to imposter syndrome. When there's a lack of mirrors—role models or people who look like you and share your background—you're especially susceptible to feeling like you don't belong.

If you're a woman in the workplace who has only ever had male managers, you'll absorb the underlying message that it will be harder, if not impossible, for you to become a manager. If you've overheard sexist or racist comments about how women don't make good leaders because they're "too emotional" or Black people "aren't good at math and science," you're more likely to internalize those beliefs. If you've had prior experience in environments where you weren't validated for your gifts, you've been primed to walk into your next job with less confidence.[11]

And, by the way: You're not making any of this up. According to a 2022 Pew Research Center analyst, women still earn an average of 82 percent of what men earn.[12] Add race to the mix and the numbers get even bleaker: Black women earn 70 percent as much as white men; Latinx women earn 65 percent as much. How can we *not* internalize the message that men are more valued by our companies and our society than women, especially women of color? Ultimately, that messaging can affect the way we feel about ourselves and the value we bring to the table.

I've met many leaders who experienced the same kind of social conditioning I did. Women of color face innumerable racial, societal, and patriarchal biases from a young age. We learn to adapt, fight, and survive. Failing is not an option. I always felt like I had something to prove; that my life had no meaning unless I really *became* somebody.

For me, this translated into an insatiable thirst for academic success. I overachieved my way through high school, college, and medical school, an exacting perfectionist who never once got a B. They don't call my personality "Type A" for nothing.

But with such ruthless expectations for myself, I never felt secure. I was terrified of getting too comfortable and slipping up. The more I succeeded, the more I felt trapped by my own success. I was constantly afraid of being "discovered," exposed as the failure I truly was. That fear only expanded as the stakes rose throughout my career. Getting a B on a high school math test is one thing; a misstep as CEO of a major biotech company is another.

Author and mental health blogger Arlin Cuncic talks about five basic ways imposter syndrome manifests. You might call them the five sub-archetypes:

- **Perfectionists** believe their best isn't good enough. If they haven't done perfectly, they've done poorly.
- **Experts** feel they don't know a lot, when in fact they do. They may have gaps in their knowledge, but they take these gaps as proof they're not knowledgeable or competent.
- **Natural Geniuses** feel like frauds because they see themselves as less intelligent than their peers. If mastering a skill takes too long, they feel like an imposter.
- **Soloists** feel that if they ever asked for help, their success is fake. They question their competence since they didn't get there entirely on their own.
- **Superpersons** believe they must work the hardest or reach the highest level possible or they're total frauds.[13]

I've known and worked with leaders in all five categories. I've watched talented individuals say no to leadership positions, accept demotions and pay cuts, and leave companies where they had bright futures. I've seen gifted professionals stuck in stasis, determined to stay where it's comfortable so they won't be exposed.

So what's the solution? How do we stop feeling like Imposters, step into our power, and claim our worth?

The answer—which you'll hear me say often—is *practice.*

At a talk at Spelman College, Michelle Obama said, "You break out of imposter syndrome by practice, work, and moving through it. Because what's the alternative? The alternative is that you're told you can't, so you quit. But every time you break through and sit at a table, you see more, learn more. You learn more about yourself—and you learn more about the system. That's how you break out of imposter syndrome."[14]

She goes on to talk about how the biggest challenge of overcoming imposter syndrome is what you repeat in your own head. "If you tell yourself you're not worthy, it's you doing it to yourself. We have to start practicing other messages. There are always going to be haters in the world—and that's true regardless of race, class, or gender. It's not about them. It's about us now."

One highly effective tool I don't hear many people talk about is **playing sports.** Team sports have long been known to build confidence and self-esteem, especially in girls. But did you know there's a positive correlation between sports and female leadership? *Ninety-four percent* of women in the C-suite played sports, half of those at the university level.[15] If you haven't played a sport in the past, it's not too late to start. Organized sports not only foster teamwork; they teach us it's okay to fail. No matter how good you are, you won't make every shot. But in the words of hockey legend Wayne Gretzky: "You miss 100 percent of the shots you don't take."[16] Once you can accept that, it's easier to pick yourself up and try again.

Perhaps the most effective, big-picture tool is to **change your mindset.** If you can get in the habit of acknowledging and celebrating your expertise and accomplishments, it will train your mind not to negate or diminish them. Stay focused on the real, tangible proof that you're not a fake. Brag on yourself. Tell people you're awesome. Take a cue from Michelle Obama, who said to those Spelman students: "I don't have imposter syndrome now, because I've been at every powerful table there is."

Reshma Saujani, founder and CEO of Girls Who Code, an international nonprofit that aims to close the gender gap in technology, has had a similar experience. She was asked to give a speech at Bill Gates's summit, to a room of Fortune 100 CEOs. She'd been given a slot between Bill Gates and Warren Buffett, and told by the event organizers that it would be particularly difficult because both men would be sitting in the front row. The organizers said that many people would be pretty intimidated by those circumstances.

But as she was sitting backstage, Saujani found herself wishing that she had been allotted *more* time, not less. And then, she thought, "How did I become *this* woman, when I used to be *that* girl?"

Over the years, she'd met so many powerful people—CEOs, presidents, prime ministers—and every time, she wound up thinking, "*You*? You're running *what*? Me and my girls, we can run circles around you."

That made her realize "it's never been about whether we're qualified, whether we're prepared, whether we're ready. That we've never really dissected all of the undeserved, unearned privilege that so many people have, and that we have literally bought and been fed basically this propaganda that we're not good enough, that we're not smart enough, that we don't belong."[17]

I've experienced my own version of this evolution. When I walk into a room now, I know how to manage my energy. I can chair a board meeting surrounded by white men, and it doesn't faze me one bit. They know they can't mess with me. My confidence comes from my medicine background, because I'm a badass drug developer. I've taken three companies public; I draw strength from these experiences. I didn't always know how to tap into that power, but these days, no one can lecture me on how to get shit done.

Is there such a thing as being overconfident? Sure. You can take any positive trait to the extreme. Some leaders wield their confidence like a weapon—we've all seen it. This creates the perfect conditions for our next archetype.

The Bitch Boss

The Bitch Boss is the polar opposite of the first archetype. Where the People-pleaser tries to appease everyone and be liked, the Bitch Boss charges boldly ahead, not caring who their actions may affect. There is, however, a connection. Reformed People-pleasers can sometimes *become* Bitch Bosses to overcompensate. They're angry and frustrated because they're so fed up. They might take on the Bitch Boss persona as a reaction to having been a doormat in the past. It's a power grab, and they ramp up the aggression to let everyone know they're nobody's chew toy.

A Bitch Boss:

- Is seen as difficult, rude, and mean
- Asks for more than they really want—or demands instead of asking
- Sets high and sometimes rigid expectations for team members, creating an environment in which people are afraid to ask for help
- Doesn't always respect their colleagues' (or anyone's) boundaries—often because they struggle to put boundaries in place for themselves
- Often surrounds themselves with more junior people or "yes-people" who validate their decisions and behaviors[18]

Simply put, a Bitch Boss is a bad and ineffective leader, no matter their gender. These leaders believe that if they're not being listened to, they must *make* others listen. Think of the mean girls in high school. They seize power via tactics that tend to be rude, immature, or petty; if someone doesn't do things the way they want, they aggressively reassert their influence. Fear is fueling every social interaction, every behavior. The people around them are afraid of incurring their wrath—no one wants to offend *The Plastics*—and that creates a toxic environment that makes it difficult to do real work.

But let's not get ahead of ourselves. You may be called a "Bitch Boss" simply for showing confident and assertive leadership, or for making unpopular but necessary decisions. In truth, you *have* to make tough decisions—and get used to being disliked—if you want to survive in the corporate world. Acting decisively doesn't make you a Bitch Boss, no matter how many people complain.

On one podcast, Meghan Markle talked about the labels people apply to women who are perceived as "difficult, which is really a code-word for the B-word."[19] Assertive women who aren't willing to conform to society's expectations are often called bitches; they have eschewed people-pleasing to step into their power.

So is it possible to reclaim the word? To find the power in it, instead of the insult?

What if we took the term "Bitch Boss"—and flipped those words around?

Nicole Lapin already did. A *New York Times*—bestselling author and serial entrepreneur, Lapin popularized the term "Boss Bitch" in her eponymous book. "A Boss Bitch is the she-ro of her own story. She is someone who takes charge of her future and embraces being a 'boss' in all aspects of the word: whether as the boss of her own life, family and career, the literal boss at work, or, as the boss of her own company."[20]

What's the difference between a Boss Bitch and a Bitch Boss? It's all about striking a balance. You must be strong and confident, able to claim your power without being overly aggressive or domineering. You want to stand your ground with the decisions you believe are right but not humiliate or punish people who disagree.

There are other terms that commonly pop up in the workplace as euphemisms. After all, most people know better than to openly call someone a bitch—at least not publicly. Many strong women leaders are accused of having "sharp elbows," a term often used to describe someone who is overbearing and abrasive.[21]

Ask a roomful of professional women how many have been told they have sharp elbows, and you'll get more than a few raised hands. It's not a term I've seen used with men—further proof of the double standard. In my experience, leaders who've been called "sharp-elbowed" are strong, no-nonsense, driven professionals. They're smart, tough, and good at their jobs.

If your elbows have ever been scrutinized, there's no harm in taking a moment to ask yourself if there's any truth in the critique. Are there times you feel you've been too pushy or demanding? Do you have unrealistic expectations for your team? Do you ever find yourself putting other people in their place to show them who's boss?

If the answer is yes, then you have work to do. Time to interrogate why you default to these attitudes and behaviors; maybe take another look at Chapter 2. Some of us go on the offense when we're attacked. When we feel doubt, insecurity, or shame, we might get reactive. We feel angry, then uncomfortable with our own anger. We lash out.

Instead of trying to avoid anger entirely, pause and ask yourself the following questions: Were you allowed to be angry as a child? Did you face consequences if you showed anger at any point in your life? Is it possible to be angry without being aggressive? Does getting angry make you a bad person?

Being assertive is vital to succeeding in the corporate world. Luckily, you can do that without pettiness or tyranny. Humiliating others to throw your weight around only makes you look weak and childish. Being a confident leader who is kind and respectful will inspire others to respect you.

If you recognize yourself in some of these Bitch Boss tendencies, whether they're actually true or just how others perceive you, here are some additional strategies to channel that strength more effectively:

- **Harness your directness consciously.** Rather than softening your communication entirely, be intentional about when and how you're direct. Save your forceful approach for truly important matters, and use a more collaborative tone for day-to-day interactions. This shows you can flex your style to fit the situation.

- **Cultivate self-awareness about your impact.** Ask trusted colleagues for honest feedback about how your communication style affects them. Consider recording yourself in meetings (with permission) to observe your tone, body language, and how much space you give others to contribute.

- **Practice mindful pauses.** Before responding in frustrating situations, take a breath. This small gap gives you time to choose your response rather than reacting from a place of defensiveness or aggression. Ask yourself: "Is this the hill I want to die on? What outcome am I trying to achieve here?"

- **Build authentic relationships.** Make time for one-on-one connections with team members where you genuinely get to know them beyond their work output. When people feel you care about them as humans, they're more likely to see your directness as helpful rather than hostile.

- **Reframe your internal narrative.** If you find yourself thinking "I have to be tough to be respected," try shifting to "I can be both kind and clear to be effective." This mental reframing helps break the false dichotomy between strength and compassion.

Remember that true power comes from bringing others along with you, not pushing them down or away. The most respected leaders combine decisiveness with genuine care for their people. By integrating these practices, you can transform how others experience your strength—moving from being feared to being both respected and trusted.

There's one last kind of leader we haven't discussed. The fourth archetype is deeply invested in their employees' success—to a fault.

The Micromanager

Micromanagers typically do excellent work. They are extremely competent and capable. They contribute the most on projects; they pay close attention to detail, probably closer than anyone else.

At first glance, that all sounds pretty good. These are consummate professionals who consistently raise the bar. So what's the problem?

Micromanagers operate on an unacknowledged truth: they don't feel they can count on other people. They must do as much as possible to get things done exactly the way they want—even if it means absorbing other people's responsibilities. Their mantra is, "I'll just take care of it myself." That leads to them feeling overtaxed, overworked, and underappreciated.

As a lifelong perfectionist, I've certainly been guilty of micromanaging. We are used to doing things the right way—or at least what we perceive to be the right way. But when we start to believe our way is the *only* way, that becomes a slippery slope. When others don't do things exactly the way we would, our tendency is to jump in and make changes.

A Micromanager:

- Needs to be copied on all team emails
- Rarely asks for outside input
- Takes pride in correcting other people's work
- Checks, double-checks, and triple-checks on deadlines
- Applies the same level of intensity and scrutiny to every task, struggling to prioritize
- Is never quite satisfied with the final product[22]

Micromanagers don't delegate tasks or train people because they don't trust anyone else. They feel a powerful need to control every aspect of every project, either because they believe no one else is competent or no one else cares. Many have spent a lifetime cleaning up other people's sloppy work, so they take over tasks preemptively to ensure that won't happen again.

But there's often something deeper going on inside the Micromanager. These leaders may be addicted to control, desperate to maintain order in the face of chaos. Maybe they came from unstable households or had to parent their parents when they were kids. They often have deep-seated insecurities and a need to prove themselves. Many Micromanagers have a poor self-image and also struggle with imposter syndrome. Because they secretly feel they don't deserve to be where they are, they assume the same about the people they supervise. That's why they're inclined to constantly look over their employees' shoulders. Since they have trouble believing in themselves, they find it difficult to believe in anyone else.

> **Don't try to learn what everyone on the team is doing.**

Like the other archetypes, being a Micromanager is often a product of your conditioning. But that doesn't mean you have to stay that way—particularly since these behaviors are undoubtedly creating more work for you and ultimately feeding into the insecurities that have made you a Micromanager in the first place.

According to *Psychology Today*, there are several ways to avoid being a Micromanager.[23] **Don't try to learn what everyone on the team is doing** at all times. Give them room to work, grow, and flourish. This not only frees up your time and energy; it builds your employees' trust in themselves and their own abilities.

Check yourself with honest reflection. Take time to identify what's driving your need to micromanage. Is it rooted in self-doubt about your own performance? Fear that mistakes will reflect poorly on you? Or perhaps past experiences where delegation went wrong?

Instead of simply telling yourself to "stop worrying," try this more practical approach:

1. Choose one project or task this week where you'll intentionally step back.

2. Set clear expectations at the beginning rather than hovering throughout.
3. Notice your urge to intervene and pause before acting on it.
4. Document positive outcomes when you've successfully delegated.

Check yourself with honest reflection.

The goal isn't to transform overnight, but to gradually build evidence that your team can succeed with appropriate guidance rather than constant oversight. Each successful delegation builds your confidence to let go more often.

The process will help you **embrace your strength as a leader.** You may feel productive managing every small detail, but all that does is demoralize the team and distract you from the tasks you should be doing. If you find yourself habitually micromanaging, try to **gradually ease up.** Instead of telling people to always CC you, ask to only be included on certain things. If you have confidence in a project, let it run without your oversight. Once you're sure the team can function without you, you can let go.

None of this is to say you should be a hands-off, devil-may-care leader who's not invested in any tasks or team members. Certain projects are critical and will need your supervision and support. But instead of jumping in as soon as you recognize a problem, wait until it's clear that people need help, *then* offer your assistance. Employees may interpret the boss stepping in as a sign something's gone wrong, so be sure to make it clear you're there to help come up with a solution, not take over or judge the work they've already done.

Lastly, **pay attention to your team's actual needs.** Don't badger them with intensive guidance when they've already got the expertise. Instead, ask people what they need, and do your best to deliver. That's how you create a healthy, thriving team—and how you become a healthy, thriving leader.

Addressing Archetypes with Mirrors

One of the most effective ways to recognize which archetypes you embody is through mirrors—trusted individuals who reflect your authentic self back to you with clarity and compassion. These mirrors are essential for seeing yourself as you truly are, rather than as the role you've been conditioned to play.

When we're trapped in limiting archetypes, we often can't see our own patterns. The People-pleaser doesn't recognize how frequently they sacrifice their needs for others

Pay attention to your team's actual needs.

or say "yes" when they desperately want to say "no." The Imposter doesn't see their legitimate accomplishments clearly, instead attributing success to luck or timing rather than their own capabilities. The Bitch Boss may not understand how their communication style affects others or recognize when they're being unfairly labeled for simply being assertive. And the Micromanager often can't see how their controlling behavior and reluctance to delegate stifles their team's creativity and growth.

This is where mirrors become invaluable. A colleague who gently points out, "I notice you apologize before sharing your ideas in meetings" helps the People-pleaser see their pattern. A mentor who mentions specific achievements when you're doubting yourself counters the Imposter's self-doubt. Someone who can distinguish between your assertiveness and actual aggression helps you navigate unfair Bitch Boss labels. And team feedback that shows how autonomy improves results can help the Micromanager loosen their grip on control.

Finding these mirrors—people who can reflect your true self without distortion—is a critical part of breaking through your inner glass ceiling. Later in this book, we'll explore in depth how to build a personal board of directors composed of these essential mirrors, but for now, consider: Who in your life helps you see beyond the archetypes you've been playing? Who reflects your authentic strengths back to you? And who compassionately shows you your blind spots?

These mirrors don't just show you what you want to see, but what you need to see to become the leader you're truly meant to be. By surrounding yourself with people who reflect your authentic self rather than the archetypes you've adopted, you create the conditions for genuine transformation and growth.

Ready to discover which archetypes you've been embodying in your professional life? *The Mirror Effect Workbook & Journal* offers reflective exercises to help you recognize your default patterns and practice stepping beyond them. Through guided self-inquiry, you'll learn to identify when you're falling into these roles and develop strategies to lead from authentic power instead.

Step into Your Power

If you're reading this book, chances are you identify with one of the four archetypes. Maybe more than one. Sometimes the best way to break old habits is to create new ones. With that in mind, I'm sharing some actionable tools to help you confront people-pleasing, imposter syndrome, aggression, and micromanagement. When you do so effectively, you can hold on to the beneficial aspects and let go of the rest, or even intentionally embody certain traits during appropriate situations to get the outcomes you want.

- **Notice the language you use—and shift it.** As we've established, naming things is powerful, as are the words we hear ourselves say—especially when they don't sync up with how we truly feel. If you identify as a People-pleaser, here are some new mantras to try. If they feel uncomfortable or scary, that might be a sign they're exactly the ones you need to practice:
  - *No.* (Fun fact: "No" is a complete sentence!)
  - *I don't have to apologize or explain myself to anyone.*
  - *My time and energy are my own.*
  - *Not my circus, not my monkeys.*

  Once you've started saying these in your own head and built up your confidence, Psych Central has some others to try out loud:
  - "I won't be able to make it."
  - "Unfortunately, I'm at capacity. I'll have to pass."
  - "I'll think about it and touch base with you tomorrow."
  - "I have plans that day but thank you for thinking of me."[24]

- **Pay attention to your posture.** If you struggle with imposter syndrome, it can be powerful to change the way you sit and stand. If you spend your days hunched over, making yourself small, you'll feel small. But if you stand tall and hold your head high, you'll feel big. Doing a "power pose" before an important board meeting can work wonders (more on that later). In the wise words of Julia Grace, VP of Product Engineering at Netflix: "Sometimes you've just got to take up space."[25]

- **Pair "sharp elbows" with a kind heart.** Most Bitch Bosses aren't actually Bitch Bosses. They're strong, assertive women who go after what they want. As a leader, you can't control the labels others put on you. What you *can* do is treat your team members with kindness and respect. Be the Boss Bitch you are destined to be.

- **Set clear boundaries from the start.** *Harvard Business Review* has some great tips for how to stop micromanaging your employees and start empowering them instead.

- **Talk about the outcome, not the process.** State what you want done, not the exact way you think it should be done. This allows the team to solve problems and refine processes on their own.

- **Set expectations around feedback.** Before a project begins, discuss when and how you'll give constructive feedback. Specify what the feedback will be, and refrain from being too detailed about less important tasks.

- **If you have a manager, talk to them about the same things you talk to your team about.** Then you can work together to build your team's trust and confidence. If you have their back, they'll be more motivated to succeed.[26]

Archetypes can serve us well in certain contexts, but they become glass ceilings within us when they limit our full potential and authentic expression. Breaking through this inner glass ceiling isn't just about recognizing which archetypes you embody—it's about consciously choosing when to inhabit them and when to step beyond them. With the help of your mirrors who reflect your true capabilities, you can shatter these self-imposed limitations that have kept you playing small.

The journey of breaking through your inner glass ceiling is ultimately a journey toward wholeness. It's about integrating all aspects of yourself—your strengths, your vulnerabilities, your expertise, and your humanity—into authentic leadership that doesn't fit neatly into any single archetype. When you free yourself from these constraining roles, you access a fuller range of your capabilities and create the space for others to do the same. This is true power—not the power that comes from controlling others or conforming to expectations, but the power that emerges when you lead from a place of authenticity, flexibility, and wholeness.

CHAPTER 4

POWERFUL BEYOND MEASURE

Seeing—and Being—Your Best Self

**"Our deepest fear is not that we are inadequate.
Our deepest fear is that we are powerful beyond measure."**

—Marianne Williamson

Before we go any further, I invite you to take a breath.
Make it a deep breath—maybe the deepest you've taken all day. Then spend a moment getting comfortable. Wherever you are, let your body settle. Once you've read the next paragraph, close your eyes and take a few minutes just for you.

Take two more deep breaths. Sip cool air through your nostrils, filling up your lungs, then exhale slowly through your mouth. Then, let the air flow in and out without trying to control it. Begin to move your awareness into your body. Each breath grounds you, connecting you more fully to the earth. Now, move your awareness up from your gut and into your heart. Spend a few moments there. Place your hands over your heart, experiencing love for yourself. Feel it pour through you, a warm and comforting glow. Then expand that love to everyone around you. **Know that you *are* love and light. You are more than enough, just as you are.**

Now open your eyes.

How'd it go? Do you feel different? Has anything shifted in your body? Your mind? Your heart?

I recently led a similar meditation in an unlikely place: at a summit for high-powered biotech executives. I was scheduled to run a breakout session, and I wanted to try something new. The lessons I'd learned over the past few years had changed how I show up in the world—both at work and at home—and I was ready to lead in a new way. This seemed like the perfect venue.

> **Know that you *are* love and light. You are more than enough, just as you are.**

The room was buzzing as I made my way to its center. An amazing group of female biotech entrepreneurs and senior executives had gathered for three days of talks, panels, and networking. The mood was positive and enthusiastic. We had come to be mirrors, to support one another, to share exciting opportunities and lift each other up.

Now, as I looked out on the faces of everyone in that conference room, I saw a cadre of smart, talented, accomplished women. The group was vibrant with diversity—and not the kind you can capture with a corporate checkbox. Women of every age, background, race, experience, and orientation sat shoulder to shoulder, hungry to collaborate and connect. The combined expertise in that room could fuel an entire industry—and frankly, it has.

When I said we were going to do a short meditation and hold space together, a murmur rippled through the crowd. I wasn't speaking to a group of yoga teachers. This was a room full of high-ranking executives—a group not historically known for "holding space." A few years ago, I would have immediately doubted myself for kicking off the weekend with something so woo-woo.

But this time, I didn't feel uncertain. I felt confident, centered, and self-assured. I had a genuine offering for these women. I knew it had the power to transform the way they felt about themselves and each other. They had come here to be open and learn. Even if this was out of their comfort zones, they were nothing if not tenacious. It was how they'd secured coveted positions at some of the best biotech companies in the world. I believed they'd lean in.

When they opened their eyes after the meditation, the energy in the room had shifted. They were present and focused in a new way. These highly intelligent women, so accustomed to relying on their intellect, were now present in their hearts and bodies, not just in their minds. They were ready for what came next.

I posed a series of questions challenging them to go deeper. To be vulnerable in a way that wasn't always safe to do in the workplace, where they were expected to be tough and thick-skinned. Then they dispersed into smaller, more intimate breakout groups and embarked on real conversations, putting to work what we'd just discussed.

When we reconvened, each group shared snippets of what they'd covered with the rest of us. They hadn't just talked about "best practices for CEOs" or effective leadership strategies. They'd talked about *life*. They shared their triumphs and challenges, frustrations and hopes. They'd opened up about health issues they were facing—infertility, menopause, illness. They'd talked about the next generation, how they wanted to create more support for the young professionals coming up in our field.

Afterward, a woman came up to me with tears in her eyes.

"I was so nervous about this weekend, I almost didn't come," she confessed. "I always feel like an imposter at these things. But after you led us in that meditation, it's like I dropped into some deeper place inside myself. I felt grounded and at peace, like I actually deserved to be here. When we did the breakout groups, I was able to show up as my true self."

I smiled. I told her she'd taken an important step today, that she absolutely belonged here, and that this inner work could change the course of her future; it had certainly changed mine. Surrounded by a support system of other women, she'd stepped into her true power. It's what I wanted for every woman in that room—and what I want for you.

I'll be posing three questions to you in the pages that follow. Questions that, a few years ago, I might not have been able to answer myself. But first, a reminder—or rather, a moment of recognition.

You Are Powerful Beyond Measure

When I was the CEO at one of my previous companies, there was a period of time where I was focused, hustling, and thriving—in my proverbial groove. I was actually building a company and doing everything I needed to do to grow a startup into a public company with an initial public offering (IPO). The result was a camaraderie-building environment and a strong, positive culture.

But I didn't really understand the impact my leadership was having on the company. I was head-down, incredibly busy running the business. I loved and thoroughly enjoyed my work; however, I still felt old fears, lingering shame, and the persistent pestilence of self-doubt. I was always worried I was two steps away from a big mistake.

I was driven to succeed, and I did. I worked long hours—longer than anyone else in the office. Now I have a more nuanced understanding that there was also an element of people-pleasing to what I was doing. When others backed off during the holiday season in favor of family gatherings and downtime, I picked up their slack. I was burning the midnight oil, giving the company more of myself than I should have. Yet I still felt self-doubt. I wasn't operating from a secure, centered place where I knew who I was and that I had nothing to prove.

The wake-up call came in the form of a holiday greeting card. It was from one of my employees, a direct report who had worked for and alongside me for years at several different companies. He'd written a heartfelt note about how proud he was of me and the leader I had become.

His words pierced my heart. The way he saw me was so different from the way I saw myself. He didn't think I was an imposter clawing my way to the top or someone who still needed to prove herself, as many of my board members had stated to me directly. He saw me as a capable, confident leader who created a successful business by sheer force of will.

At the end of his note, he shared an excerpt from Marianne Williamson's book *A Return to Love*, including the famous quote: "Our deepest fear is not that we are inadequate. Our deepest fear is that we are powerful beyond measure. It is our light, not our darkness that most frightens us."[1]

I was deeply touched. Was it true? Was I powerful beyond measure? Is that how others perceived me? Would I ever be able to step into that power—or was I too frightened to find out?

For the first time, I saw myself through someone else's eyes. I *was* that powerful. I *was* creating a successful business by sheer force of will. I had *already* stepped into my power without even realizing it. I built this company, brought this team together, and created this success. *Wow.*

That short poetic excerpt shook me out of chronic self-criticism and pulled me back from the grindstone. And for the first time, I started to see past my self-limiting beliefs, the fear and shame I'd lugged around my whole life. Those three sentences shifted something inside me. Suddenly, I felt a newfound sense of deep peace and comfort. It was like wiping down a mirror that had always been cloudy. When I looked into the clean glass, I saw *me.*

I had co-founded a company and cultivated a positive environment where people could learn from their mistakes and support one another. I had a great work ethic—an ethic that my bosses and mentors had often exploited to their own advantage. But I was damn good at my job. I was a badass CEO.

I was also a good mom. I wasn't perfect—I made a million mistakes—but I loved my kids and showed up for them. They knew how important they were to me. Even when my career was extremely demanding, they were always my top priority.

I started to make a list of what I had accomplished and what I was good at. I listed out medical therapies I had developed that were treating patients all over the world, along with my other professional successes. To my surprise, I kept adding more and more line items. I had greatness inside me. Untapped potential. A power I'd been too afraid to name. Until my employee held up a mirror and gave me the gift of his perspective, I hadn't seen it. I'd been hiding that greatness for a long time—and hiding my true self in the process.

So how was I going to fully step out of the darkness and into the light? At the beginning, I didn't have a clue. What kind of tools did I need to begin a serious self-excavation? How was I going to free my latent power from years of damaging patterns, conditioning, gaslighting, and toxic environments? Were there practical ways to chip away at the fear, insecurity, and shame that had crystallized in every crevice of my life?

Everyone's path is different; different strokes for different folks. But each path passes through the powerful lessons I've learned: *Love yourself. Be your authentic self. Follow your passion.* And the best way I've found to weave these lessons into my daily life is by practicing the Three Cs: **compassion, centering,** and **celebration.**

Cultivate Self-Compassion

Question 1: *Do you show yourself the same compassion you show the people you love?*

Showing yourself compassion can be surprisingly hard to do. For most of us, it's far easier to be compassionate toward others.

Author and self-compassion expert Dr. Kristin Neff has been making the case for self-compassion for the past two decades. Rather than focusing on self-esteem, she argues that prioritizing self-compassion is more useful. For Neff, self-compassion means "treating yourself with the same kind of kindness, care, compassion, as you would treat those you care about—your good friends, your loved ones."[2]

Take a moment to call to mind a person who meets those criteria. It could be a friend, family member, or someone else in your life you feel close to. The only requirement is that you adore this person. You think they hung the moon.

Now imagine something you've said to yourself on your worst day. I'm talking about the messages that parade through our heads, whispering our darkest fears. *Who do you think you are? You're such an embarrassment. Everyone is laughing at you. They're going to find out you're a fraud. No matter how hard you try, you're just going to fail.*

Now take those exact same words—and imagine directing them to the person you adore.

Hard to imagine, right? The person I call to mind is my teenage daughter. When I imagine speaking to her this way, it's physically painful. I would never say these things to her. So why do I think it's okay to say them to myself?

Now, flip the paradigm. Conjure up your person again, but this time, shower them in kindness. Speak to them the way you do naturally, with the love and respect you know they deserve. *You are doing an amazing job. How are you so brilliant? You're absolutely killing it today. You slay in that pantsuit. I'm so glad you're in the world.*

Now Say Those Same Words To Yourself

This has been a very powerful practice for me: speaking to myself—and treating myself—the way I speak to and treat my daughter. When I do this, everything shifts. I will tell her she's amazing until my last breath. When she encounters challenges or adversity, I am always on her side. If she messes up or makes a mistake, I love and accept her just as much as when she succeeds. I remind her she's doing the best she can; that she is strong and capable and *already* perfect. Though people will try to shape her into what they want her to be, the choice is ultimately and always hers. And when I echo those words back to myself, I see things in a new light.

I am also fortunate to have an amazing daughter who actually sends me texts like these (yes, in all caps): "TOTAL GIRLBOSS. YOU SLAY

SO HARD EVERY SINGLE PERSON THERE IS LITERALLY DEAD." Those messages are usually followed by "will u be home for dinner?" Or "Love you girly keep slayqueening remember you are a girlboss light it up girlypop!" . . . followed by a string of emoji. I am forced to search the web for many of the terms she uses to fully grasp her messages, but they make me soar.

In my own journey, I've found that combining self-reflection practices with regular sessions with executive coaches and therapists creates a powerful synergy. While journaling allows for self-examination, having skilled professionals who can help you interpret and work through what surfaces in those reflections accelerates your growth exponentially. My coaches have helped me recognize patterns I couldn't see on my own and offered strategies tailored to my specific challenges as a woman of color in leadership.

Write It Down

Another tool I've found immensely helpful is keeping **a self-compassion journal**.[3] Dr. Neff suggests trying this practice for just one week. If you find it useful, you can always keep going. Personally, I don't plan to stop anytime soon.

This kind of journaling isn't about opening to a fresh page every morning and writing down ten things that make you amazing. (Though that's great, too!) It's more about getting honest with yourself and doing the daily work of disentangling habits and thought patterns that don't serve you. In fact, Neff suggests journaling in the evening, if you're able to snatch a quiet ten minutes to reflect on the events of the day. Write down anything you feel bad about: any moments that caused you pain, guilt, or made you judge yourself.

Maybe Ted, one of your employees, was late submitting a report, so you didn't have what you needed before a board meeting. You were justifiably upset, but you didn't want to be accused of being "mean" or having "sharp elbows." So instead of engaging in an honest conversation with Ted about what happened, you simmered about it quietly . . . and then took all the blame and fell all over yourself apologizing to the board. Afterward, you felt furious at Ted for letting you down and angry at yourself for once again taking ownership of other people's mistakes just to keep the peace.

If you're like me, you stew over these situations all day, feeling increasingly ashamed. You say to yourself, *Why couldn't I just . . . ?* More often than not, this spiraling doesn't help you *or* the person you feel has wronged you. It merely sends you reeling into a panicked state of fear and worry, exacerbating all the patterns you're trying to break.

The goal of keeping a self-compassion journal is to break this cycle. When you journal about difficult events, you make a conscious choice to cultivate self-compassion. To do that, Neff recommends viewing them through the lens of mindfulness, common humanity, and kindness.

- The special sauce at the root of **mindfulness** is awareness. Before we can disarm the bomb of self-judgment, we have to coax our authentic feelings to the surface. How are you feeling about what happened? Ashamed? Embarrassed? Defeated? Try not to judge these feelings as they come up—just identify them.

  You might write in your journal, "I was frustrated because it's not the first time Ted has turned in a report late, and the last time it happened it made me look bad. But because I was afraid of upsetting the apple cart and being called a Bitch Boss, I decided to take ownership of a problem that wasn't mine. The result was threefold: I felt angry that Ted hadn't delivered, ashamed to get my hand slapped by the board, and furious at myself that I kept putting myself in these lose-lose situations."

- Neff says self-compassion "also entails a recognition of **common humanity**—in other words, the understanding that all people are imperfect, and all people have imperfect lives."[4] Now that you've identified your feelings, write about the ways your experience connects to the larger human experience. This could include a universal statement like, "Everyone takes the blame sometimes for things that aren't their fault." Or a slightly more tailored: "It's completely normal to want to keep the board happy, especially when I'm a woman of color answering to eight white men."

You could even write about the extenuating circumstances or influencing factors around the event. "This morning, I was running late getting the kids out the door for school, and I snapped at them for something that wasn't their fault. I felt terrible about it, so when I took all the blame for Ted's blunder, I think I was partly trying to punish myself for being a 'bad mom.' If I'd had a different morning, I might have been able to react from a more calm, centered place."

- Now that you've started seeing things in a new light by tapping into other perspectives, it's time to harness the energy of **self-kindness.** Build off the earlier exercise and write some words of comfort you might say to your daughter, sister, or best friend. Let your tone be gentle and reassuring. "It's okay. You've spent a long time people-pleasing, and in many ways, it's gotten you where you are in your career. You had a rough morning, and it spilled over into some long-standing habits. Makes complete sense. But you're doing a great job. You're learning how to lead in a new way. Maybe next time Ted drops the ball, you can practice how to be kind, not nice, and not take responsibility for what isn't yours."

Dr. Neff offers a whole series of exercises on her website, self-compassion.org, an outstanding resource for weaving more self-compassion into your life.[5] I can't recommend them highly enough.

Do you see how this practice is powerful and profound? Bit by bit, you're rewriting the narrative. All the negative ways you think about and talk to yourself begin to loosen their hold as you call in more kindness and understanding. When we view our actions and reactions as normal human experiences, we can grow. When we view them as abnormal, we end up blaming ourselves. One of the greatest gifts of self-compassion is to remind us we are not alone. Once you begin to see your life as part of a collective human experience, it's easier to love yourself the way you love others. *And this is essential: to truly love yourself.*

If journaling isn't for you, here's another empowering tool: **write yourself a love letter.** It could be one line. "Dear Sheila: Today you did something that made me proud." Or if you've got more time, write a whole page. Talk about the ways you're growing, your hopes and desires, and what you wish for yourself. Practice deep empathy with phrases like, "I'm sorry you had to go through that. It sounds so hard."

You don't have to shy away from your imperfections but write about them with tenderness and genuine support. "I saw how hard you tried to impress the investors in that meeting today. Remember that you don't have to prove yourself to anyone. You're worthy whether they invest or not." I know from my own experience it is possible to replace the critical, judgmental voices with loving, compassionate ones. It just takes time and practice. And as you get better at accessing self-compassion, you'll be better equipped to practice the second of the Three Cs.

Return to Center

Question 2: *When the world around you is chaotic and cutthroat, what do you do to center yourself?*

Think of a time you've felt centered. Maybe you were hiking out in nature. Maybe you were sweating it out at the gym. Maybe you and your kids were enjoying a fun family game night. Maybe you were standing at the kitchen counter, soothed by the steady rhythm of chopping vegetables for a stew.

There are as many ways to center yourself as there are dinner recipes. The exercise I offered at the beginning of this chapter is one tool, but what works for me may not work for you. The important thing is that you build a tool kit to help you feel calm and grounded. If you've already got some tools in that kit, fantastic. You can always add a few more. And if your tool kit is looking pretty empty, that's fine. It might take a little experimentation to find the stuff that lights you up inside, but those experiments could become the most empowering science project you ever do.

Here's one to get you started. Think of a majestic throne room. Perhaps you've visited a palace or castle and seen a historic replica. Maybe you were a fan of *Game of Thrones*. Whatever the case, ask yourself this: Is the throne ever shoved to one side of the room or hidden in the wings? No. It's the heart of the throne room, the focal point, the seat of power. And that's not just true for Daenerys on the Iron Throne; it can be true for you, too. When you find your center, you feel that power. And that means you're far less inclined to doubt yourself or feel like an imposter. On the contrary: you are ready to rule.

A good ruler always takes the time to observe the goings-on in their domain. When you can manage your energy, you can start to observe all the intrusive thoughts and limiting beliefs clogging up your mind. You might even **call out the negative voices** that pull you off course, because you are in control.

One way to accomplish this is through a therapeutic modality called "cognitive defusion" in which you separate yourself from your thoughts.[6] Cognitive defusion helps you look *at* your thoughts rather than *through* them. To engage in that separation, you can give those thoughts a name—the sillier the better. I've found this very helpful. When the voice in my head starts to tell me my employees hate me, or I'm going to mess up in that board meeting, or I'll never be good enough, I sometimes say out loud, "Hey, Negative Nancy. You're not being helpful, and I don't appreciate your tone. Would you talk to your best friend that way?"

If it feels too weird to say out loud, write it down in your journal. Putting those harmful thoughts in someone else's voice gets them out of your own head. I often feel physically lighter afterward, like I've shucked off a weight that's been holding me down.

But maybe attempting cognitive defusion techniques yourself isn't enough. Maybe there's more behind those negative thoughts than you're equipped to deal with on your own. Many of us survived traumatic experiences in our childhood or adolescence. The lasting effects may be obvious, or they may lurk in our subconscious, waiting to trip us up. Because most of us don't have the specific skill set to source and heal our own trauma—especially wounds we suffered in childhood—the best path to healing is often to **work with a therapist.** These highly trained professionals can help you rewire your thinking. I once mentored a young woman of color who said the first time she felt truly centered was during a breakthrough therapy session when she realized her past experiences didn't have to define her. Not anymore.

In addition to counseling and therapy, there are plenty of simple tools you can practice at home on your own, such as **positive affirmations.** These are exactly what they sound like: affirming phrases, inspirational words, and motivational quotes that are meaningful to you. I have friends who keep affirmations in their purses, on their desks, on Facebook or Instagram, or taped to their bathroom mirrors. Every time you see those words, you get a fresh chance to repeat them back to yourself, absorbing their power. And before you relegate affirmations to the realm of the woo-woo, I'll tell you that multiple studies have shown the power of positive thinking. Affirming words can bolster your sense of self-worth, minimize stress in the body, and improve your ability to cope with difficult experiences.[7]

Affirmations aren't just for wealthy white women, either. In one illuminating social-psychological study, Black students who showed an elevated level of psychological threat from negative stereotypes were given writing assignments to reaffirm their "sense of personal adequacy and self-integrity." Afterward, their grades significantly improved, reducing the racial achievement gap by 40 percent.[8]

Again, it's all about experimenting to find what's right for you. Gardening might be your favorite way to get centered, whereas it stresses me out. Give me a quiet room and meditation cushion any day.

Speaking of which, there's plenty of excellent research on the positive effects of **meditation**. Scientists at Harvard have proven meditation can actually change the brain, specifically in the amygdala. These neurological changes may explain meditation's effectiveness in treating depression and anxiety.[9] You don't even have to sit on your cushion every day to reap the benefits. Studies have shown that brain activity in people who have learned to meditate holds steady, even when they're not meditating. Talk about rewiring your brain!

My meditation practice helps bring me back to myself. When the storms come—and they will inevitably come—I draw from a deep well of calm and courage. As a *sadhika* (a spiritual practitioner or seeker), I have a *sadhana* (a dedicated spiritual practice aimed at personal transformation), which is simply a means of growth. I view my professional and personal life as one unified experience. I don't want to be two different people; I want to live an authentic, integrated life. So, I practice mindful self-compassion in all the roles I play—CEO, entrepreneur, mentor, mom. I'm not shooting for perfection. The goal is growth.

These centering practices may be simple, but they're not easy. It's hard to return to center when we're trying to be excellent leaders and inspiring mentors and good parents. So, I encourage you to rewrite the story: to *challenge* our cultural narrative of what success means. And do so in a way that supports your journey. When you find your center amidst all the noise, it's a triumph, not a failure. Celebrate it.

Which brings us to the third C.

Celebrate Yourself

Question 3: *How do you acknowledge your wins?*

We all know the feeling: You just got promoted, or you've made it to the final round of interviews for your dream job, or you have big news to share. You snap a quick photo of the evidence and head over to LinkedIn or Instagram. You're brimming with excitement, eager to update your friends and professional connections.

And then, you hesitate. You scroll down your feed, index finger hovering over the trackpad. Should you *really* share your good news? What if people think you're bragging? Maybe it's better not to draw attention. You should probably just go about your work and keep your wins to yourself.

Multiple studies have shown that women generally have a harder time than men acknowledging their achievements and promoting themselves within an organization. An *Harvard Business Review* study found a substantial gender gap in self-promotion: "Women systematically provide less favorable assessments of their own past performance and potential future ability than equally performing men."[10]

Here's my hot take: This isn't your fault. Our reticence to visibly champion ourselves is not a personal failing; it's a completely rational response to how we've been taught to conduct ourselves in the workplace and the world.

In a *Forbes* workplace study, 1,200 participants—almost all women—were asked if they were actively taking steps to make people aware of their accomplishments. Only 60 percent said yes. "In some organizations," writes researcher Jo Miller, "women face an exasperating double bind: self-advocate, and be sidelined for lacking social skills. Fail to self-advocate, and have your competence questioned." When Miller asked participants to cite the challenges they faced, the number one most common challenge was "having their value and contributions recognized."[11]

Sound familiar? We've found yet another example of the pervasive cultural conditioning we've all internalized. And it isn't just women. A National Library of Medicine study indicated that Black employees who promoted their work were rated "less favorably" on job performance than their white, Latinx, and Asian colleagues.[12]

Why is it so hard for us to celebrate ourselves? Maybe because everything in our external environment is screaming, DON'T!

There's no easy solution. But here's my suggestion for how to navigate it: **Indulge in self-celebration whenever and wherever you can.**

Indulge in self-celebration whenever and wherever you can.

I call it self-celebration because that name creates a distinction between external praise and the celebrating you do for only yourself. You don't need anyone else to validate how great you are because you know it already—even if it doesn't translate to the new role or a promotion you deserve.

I'm not saying you don't have a right to be frustrated when you are qualified for a position but get passed over or pushed aside. You have every right to be angry, and to fight the flawed system. But if you can find ways to stand firm in your sense of self and acknowledge your own greatness, that fight will be easier to win.

So when something positive happens in your life or career, **post on LinkedIn and social media.** When I receive an award or public acknowledgement for my contributions in biotech, I share it. I encourage others to do the same. If your colleagues, acquaintances, or friends don't like it? They're not the support system you need.

When you celebrate yourself, you also get a chance to **be a mirror for others, inspiring the people around you** to celebrate their own triumphs. I get notes all the time from women and people of color thanking me for sharing my successes because it emboldened them to share theirs. They tell me, "You achieved this dream, Sheila. So maybe I can, too."

I'm not saying you should make everything a Me Parade. The vast majority of my posts aren't about me at all. I boost other people. I highlight leaders who inspire me. I share valuable insights and ideas I've learned from things I've read or conversations I've had with friends and colleagues. When you're intentional in how you use self-celebration, it extends far beyond yourself. You've created a dynamic, healthy exchange where you celebrate others and they celebrate you.

When you start to celebrate yourself, casting off your fears of sounding braggy or egotistical, *you'll find that other people are ready to celebrate you, too.* They become your true champions, which is so vital when so many of us struggle to champion ourselves.

> To incorporate the Three Cs into your daily life, *The Mirror Effect Workbook & Journal* provides specific practices for cultivating self-compassion, finding your center, and celebrating your accomplishments. These structured reflections help you build the habit of treating yourself with the same kindness you show others and embracing your inherent power.

Which brings us to my fourth and final question.

Question 4: *Are you enough for yourself?*

As is the case with most brilliant questions, this one came from Oprah.

It goes without saying that Oprah is a true legend and one of the most successful women in the world. Part of her brand—and the way she uses her power—is to give back, helping members of historically marginalized communities find and amplify their voices. At a recent class she taught at the California Correctional Women's Institute, she asked her students to write essays on who they are versus who they're meant to be.

"The essays were so powerful, poignant, heartbreaking, and shattering," Oprah shared in her *Daily Insider.* "One inmate wrote of years of abuse as a child developing into lack of trust. She said, 'How can you trust someone if you can't trust your own parents?' And then being incarcerated for over twenty-seven years and finally coming to the realization that the thing that she'd been searching for, longing for, committing crime after crime for was to feel worthy and to feel enough . . . that's the ultimate question I think for all of us.

"Have you reached a point in your life where you're not trying to live up to other people's expectations, trying to satisfy their needs or their desires, and have learned to trust yourself enough to be enough for you?"[13] she asks.

If your answer is "No," that's okay. For most of us, it's an ongoing process. Your answer may fluctuate by the day, if not the hour. If self-compassion, centering, and celebrating yourself are all new muscles, go easy on yourself. You don't go straight from a walk around the neighborhood to running a marathon. You train. You practice. You fall down and get up again. You condition your brain and body in an entirely different way than the conditioning you've been prescribed. It's the same with reclaiming your power: Step by step, you are teaching yourself to be the best you can be.

Being the best isn't about racking up the most awards or scaling the corporate ladder. Do I believe you deserve to be recognized and rewarded? Absolutely. The irony is that, once you let go of needing external accolades to prove your worth, you're more likely to achieve them, as are the people around you. Leaders who channel their authentic power are a force to be reckoned with—and a rising tide lifts all boats.

We opened this chapter with a simple meditation. I'll offer you another one to close. Take three deep breaths. I've shared a lot of tools and resources in this chapter, which can be overwhelming. Give yourself a moment to let them settle as you ground yourself. Give them space and see if any drop from your mind and down into your body. Your heart.

Which ones call to you? Are there specific offerings that feel like they're taking root? Let instinct and intuition run the show. You may be called to one or three or five. There might even be some that scare you. Don't run from those. The things that scare us can be our greatest teachers. Sometimes the tools that feel most challenging—the ones that make you go, "Oh, I could never do *that*"—bear the most fruit.

When you open your eyes again, take a few minutes to jot down what rose to the surface during this meditation. Let that list guide you. And by the way: Congratulations. You just wrote a customized road map for how to be your best self.

Step into Your Power

The internet has no shortage of ideas for how to practice the Three Cs. To borrow a term from biotech, do a little R&D (research and development). You might:

- **Try yoga**, a practice that's both physical and spiritual and has all sorts of benefits beyond the mat.[14]
- **Write "morning pages,"** a term coined by multi-hyphenate Julia Cameron in her book *The Artist's Way*—a practice of jotting down three pages of longhand, stream-of-consciousness writing first thing in the morning to clear mental clutter and unlock creativity before you start the day.[15]
- **Give yourself a recess**, a way to play outside of—or perhaps *inside* of—typical working hours. Cameron is an advocate of a practice she calls "Artist Dates," a way to carve out time for yourself to refill your creative well.[16]
- **Exercise.** We all know the benefits of working out, even if we struggle to actually do it! According to the CDC, just 150 minutes of moderate physical activity every week can work wonders.[17] That's only twenty-one

minutes a day. All things considered, that's a pretty quick hack to get centered.

- **Garden**. As I've confessed, not my top choice and not an activity that makes me feel a lot of self-compassion. But if you're someone who feels calm holding a shovel and digging around in the dirt, be my guest.
- **Take a walk** in nature. Nature can be soothing for many of us; others might prefer a leisurely stroll through an art museum or a jaunt through a big, bustling city. A bonus perk of walking if you can increase speed: You're sneaking in some physical exercise, too.
- **Mentor a young professional** in your field. When I show up authentically for my mentees, I feel a tremendous amount of peace and satisfaction, like I'm connected to my purpose. We'll talk more about mentorship later.
- **Give people a shout-out** when they share good news. If you see a post where a friend or colleague has drummed up the courage to celebrate their successes, don't just scroll past it. Consider reposting or posting your own.
- **Make it a regular practice to celebrate yourself.** You could even set a reasonable target, i.e., you'll post once a month about an accomplishment that makes you proud. As you get more comfortable, consider posting more frequently. Maybe you ramp up to once every two weeks, or even weekly. If that feels like too much self-promotion, you can always scale it back.

Remember, you don't have to be perfect at any of these right away. You don't have to be perfect, ever! The goal is to nudge yourself out of your comfort zone, finding fresh and supported ways to be more compassionate, more centered, more celebrated.

You are not inadequate, even if it's how you've felt your whole life. Even if it's what the world has whispered in your ear, prompting you to hide your best self from others—and from yourself. Quite the opposite. You are more than good enough. You are powerful beyond measure.

We've talked about how to know yourself and claim your power, since every epic journey starts internally. Now it's time to put that power into practice out in the world. Next up: delving into knowing and navigating your environment.

PART II

REFLECT ON YOUR SURROUNDINGS: UNDERSTAND YOUR ENVIRONMENT

CHAPTER 5

UNCHARTED TERRITORY
Navigating Difficult Work Environments

"The most rage-provoking element of being a female is the gaslighting that happens when for centuries we've been expected to absorb male behavior silently."

–*Taylor Swift*

So now you know the truth: you are powerful beyond measure—and you've begun the internal work of stepping into that power. You are confronting your fears and dismantling years of doubt and limiting beliefs. You know that to be your *best* self, you must connect to your *authentic* self, so you're cultivating self-compassion, becoming more centered, and celebrating your successes. Most importantly, you know who you really are—and no one can take that away from you.

They can, however, try.

Part I was about knowing yourself. Part II is about knowing your environment. We often can't control our surroundings, especially once we've reached the upper echelons of a company. But there are things we *can* control: ourselves and our reactions. We don't want to carry around resentment. We can improve our ability to understand and respond to a challenging situation; to read the room and the people inside it. If we want to thrive as leaders, it is essential that we hone these skills.

As you move into positions of leadership, you'll be dealing with more powerful—and potentially more difficult—personalities. The political landscape of an organization can look markedly different at the top than the one you glimpsed as you ascended. Yes, leadership sets the tone. There's certainly a trickle-down effect in company cultures. But when you take on a senior executive or board-level role, you're in a different environment, dealing with highly sophisticated individuals who play by different rules.

As a woman and person of color, I used to feel insecure when I walked into these environments. Many of us do. We typically go in one of two directions: react or retreat.

In the former case, we may be on high alert, easily agitated, questioning whether we truly belong. As a result, we don't act from a centered, thoughtful place; we're too busy reacting to what's going on around us.

In the latter case, we may be so focused on wanting to prove ourselves that we automatically morph to fit our surroundings, regardless of how toxic they are. We feel uncomfortable, but that's nothing new—we've rarely felt like we belonged, even as kids. Our cultural, racial, and familial backgrounds conditioned us to retreat; we've spent years getting comfortable feeling uncomfortable. So we train ourselves to keep calm and carry on. We work hard, keep our heads down, and refuse to rock the boat, even when the waters become unbearably choppy.

I've seen many brilliant leaders advance through the ranks of their companies. They take on senior positions where they'll be influencing, managing their boards, and making decisions that carry a lot of weight. At first, they tackle their roles with excitement and vigor. This is exactly what they've been preparing for, sometimes their whole lives!

But fast forward a year and that vigor has evaporated. They've been using all the same skills that got them from there to here—and something's not working. They feel isolated and alone. All the old doubt and insecurity has come creeping back. Suffice it to say, they're not in Kansas anymore.

In my career, I've heard all sorts of colorful ways to describe these environments. We're surrounded by sharks or walking into a den of snakes. A fellow female board member once warned me there were snipers on the board.

Nobody *wants* to work with sharks, snakes, or snipers. You may choose to enact the "No Asshole Rule"—more on that in the next chapter—and walk away. You certainly wouldn't be alone. As the saying goes: People don't quit a job; they quit a boss. According to a Gallup study, 50 percent of employees have left their jobs at some point to get away from their managers.[1] Sometimes that's just what you must do to maintain your sanity and happiness. The goal, then, is to put yourself in the strongest position to find your next role at your next company. If you have to leave, make sure you leave on your own terms.

In other situations, or at other points in your career, you may choose to stay. In those cases, you must adopt a new mindset. The people you're dealing with in these more powerful roles may be gruff; they may have biases; they may be old school. But you can choose how you respond to them. Even if you can't control their behavior, you can learn to better understand them and why they act the way they do.

Everyone is suffering. That's what I've come to understand on my own spiritual journey. We've all been conditioned by our families, cultures, and professional experiences. Every human on earth is dealing with FIDS—fear, insecurity, doubt, shame—in their own way. When someone is an asshole, it's about them, not you. But we still have to deal with one another. We still have to learn to navigate complex environments to set ourselves up for success.

In this chapter, we'll dive into three environments leaders often encounter at an organization's highest levels: a fear-based workplace, a cutthroat competitive culture, and an environment where you are being actively gaslit. We'll talk about how each of these places looks and feels—and how to assess the situation, find true allies, and take action.

First, let's walk through the markers of each environment and discuss how they might impact you as a leader and the people you supervise.

When Fear Trumps Psychological Safety

We all know what it's like to work in an environment steeped in fear. If there's a bully at the top—or more likely, several—the ethos of bullying might be baked into the company culture. In these organizations, there's no space to be vulnerable or ask questions, no room to make mistakes.

The irony of fear-based environments is that the more people are patrolled and punished, the less successful the company will be. There is more than a quarter century of research on how the way people feel at work impacts their performance. Fear inhibits all kinds of outcomes that leaders want. According to Wharton management professor Stephanie Creary, "Fear can manifest into anxiety, depression, and hopelessness, and an environment in which these negative emotions are prevalent can become a very hard one to work in and be productive. Hope, on the other hand, can breed happiness, confidence, and all sorts of positive emotions that are much more tied to positive performance and well-being."[2]

In his book *Speak-Up Culture*, Stephen Shedletzky talks about how to foster an environment where people feel heard and know that their opinions and contributions matter.[3] He argues that every leader has a responsibility to create this kind of environment. Organizations with speak-up cultures are safer, more innovative, more engaged, and better-performing than cultures where people are afraid to show up as their authentic selves.

Much has been written about team psychological safety in the workplace. *Harvard Business Review* defines it as "a shared belief held by members of a team that it's okay to take risks, to express their ideas and concerns, to speak up with questions, and to admit mistakes—all without fear of negative consequences."[4] It's a key ingredient if people are going to learn, thrive, and do their best. People won't speak up if they know they'll be made fun of or belittled. I've been in environments where leaders ridicule anyone who asks a question. These are textbook bullies, the kind of people who enjoy making others feel stupid and small.

Psychological safety is particularly vital when building diverse teams. A Harvard study zeroed in on a single industry: drug development, which happens to be my bailiwick. The results showed that "psychological safety may be the key to realizing the promise of diversity in teams."[5] That safety isn't just a nice bonus—it has a powerful impact on innovation and performance.

A recent McKinsey survey showed that "when employees feel comfortable asking for help, sharing suggestions informally, or challenging the status quo without fear of negative social consequences, organizations are more likely to innovate quickly, unlock the benefits of diversity, and adapt well to change." Unfortunately, that's not the norm. The research was clear: a positive team climate has a strong effect on psychological safety. And yet, only 43 percent of respondents reported a positive climate within their team.[6]

Let's imagine Amira, a mid-level product manager at a tech company. She's brilliant—with deep expertise in user experience and data analytics that could transform her company's flagship product. Yet in team meetings, she finds herself holding back crucial feedback. Her supervisor, Marcus, has a habit of dismissing suggestions with subtle eyerolls or interruptions, especially when those suggestions come from women on the team.

During a critical product review, Amira notices a significant flaw in the user flow that could impact retention metrics. She hesitates, remembering how Marcus publicly shut down her colleague's input last week. When she finally musters the courage to speak up, Marcus immediately shifts the conversation: "Let's stick to the agenda." The message is clear: challenging ideas aren't welcome.

Six months later, after launch, the exact issue Amira identified emerges as the primary reason for poor adoption. In the post-mortem meeting, Marcus asks, "Why didn't anyone catch this earlier?" The irony is palpable as team members exchange knowing glances but remain silent.

This scenario plays out daily in organizations worldwide. Fear-based environments don't just stifle individual voices; they fundamentally compromise business outcomes. When psychological safety is absent, organizations lose the invaluable perspectives of their diverse talent, particularly from those already navigating bias in the workplace. The cost isn't just emotional; it directly impacts innovation, productivity, and ultimately, the bottom line.

Safety should be a fundamental pillar of every organization. But as we'll see in Chapter 6, although bullies often try to control others through fear, the real irony is that they are usually battling deep fears of their own. They rarely express them, terrified of being seen as vulnerable. And yet, when we peel back the layers of bullying and fear-mongering, we begin to see that these are wounded people, too.

When Healthy Competition Turns Cutthroat

I once worked at a company where every board meeting felt like a battle. "Well *that* was a good meeting," we'd say afterward. "But there are dead bodies everywhere."

Some companies are known for having an aggressive, take-no-prisoners approach. They might even tout it as a good thing. "We're not afraid to play hardball." "Go out there and crush the competition." "Let's outflank our competitors." "We're going to make a preemptive strike." Let the sports and war metaphors abound.[7]

The problem with a brutally competitive, winner-takes-all culture is that you live in constant fear of being the loser. One misstep, one failure, and you might become a company casualty. Your colleagues no longer feel like players on the same team.

To be clear: I'm not against competition. "A little friendly competition can offer a boost of creativity and innovation," says *Forbes*.[8] "Competition motivates people to achieve more, to push past their limits," says *Entrepreneur*.[9] I completely agree!

The problem arises when a healthy sense of competition turns toxic. People feel pitted against each other. Incentives aren't implemented well, creating what feels like a carrot-and-stick situation—some employees are rewarded while others are punished. The organization foments raw, unbridled competition with no checks and balances, an atmosphere that encourages rivalry instead of collaboration—and comes at a cost.

Competitive environments create the conditions for a kind of ruthlessness that is damaging to everyone involved. Some competitors play dirty. They say there are no feelings in the mix; that it isn't personal. If they feel threatened that you'll pull ahead in the race, they're not afraid to take you down.

Let's say you've experienced some version of this in a past position. You once enjoyed the incentives and bonuses you received, but eventually you were plagued by constant worry that you were falling behind while others sprinted ahead. You talked to several colleagues about it. They, too, felt worried and stressed. So, you tried to address the situation by talking to company leadership.

Instead of listening, they shut you down. "Everyone here enjoys a little healthy competition," they told you. "You're the only one complaining." After this conversation, you noticed subtle shifts in the way they spoke to you. You felt you were being penalized in a hundred little ways, but no one would acknowledge it.

Someone turned the gaslight on.

When the Gaslight Goes On

The term "gaslight" originates from the 1940s psychological thriller *Gas Light* starring Ingrid Bergman, Charles Boyer, and a teenaged Angela Lansbury in her first film role. In the movie, a husband launches a campaign of abuse against his wife to make her question her sanity. He secretly removes pictures from the walls and tells her she imagined the changes; makes noises in the boarded-up attic so she thinks she's hearing things; and—here's the kicker—installs gas lamps that dim without being touched. His goal? To make her lose her mind.

Gaslighting has become a popular term in the zeitgeist, where it's taken on more heft. Gaslighting occurs when someone deliberately manipulates you over time, making you question your own reality. It's an insidious form of control where they systematically undermine your perceptions, memories, and experiences until you no longer trust your own judgment. You start second-guessing yourself, feeling confused about what's actually happening, and losing confidence in your ability to interpret events correctly. It erodes your self-esteem and leaves you doubting your emotional and mental stability. This psychological tactic is particularly dangerous because it's often subtle and happens gradually, making it difficult to recognize until you're deep in its grip.

You might recognize that feeling of having small bits of your power peeled away, day after day—and no one acknowledges it. The countless microaggressions. Feeling reactive and not knowing why. The off-color jokes you feel obliged to endure or deflect with a smile. The rude comment you think about for days afterward. And when you finally get up the nerve to ask your colleague what they meant, they deny saying it at all.

Gaslighters may pretend to be your friends, but they will never be your allies. They're sneaky and untrustworthy, slithering quietly through their environment, spreading their venom in various ways. Maybe it's malicious gossip. Maybe it's subtle sabotage. Or maybe it's a complete, career-altering betrayal—one they then pretend never occurred.

Consider Rena, a woman of color who's been preparing to step into a senior executive role. She's had multiple conversations with her mentor and the board about the position so she feels ready for the new challenges and responsibilities it entails. In fact, Rena's responsibilities are already expanding. She's essentially performing all the requisite duties that go with the job—and doing them beautifully. And yet the title, authority, and fair compensation have yet to materialize.

Months go by. A full year. Whenever she asks about it, she never gets a straight answer. She's repeatedly told, "We already discussed this." Demoralized, Rena starts to doubt herself. Questions begin percolating in her mind. *Am I being overly ambitious? Do people think I'm acting entitled? Maybe I misread things. I must be remembering wrong.* Meanwhile, she continues to be manipulated into doing more without recognition or reward. When the company promotes one of her colleagues into the C-suite—a guy named John who has a decade less experience and two fewer degrees—she feels understandably betrayed.

An article in the *Harvard Business Review* suggests that gaslighting is a "particularly nefarious form of toxicity due to its subtle and insidious nature. While it is easy to spot toxic leaders who scream, bully, and abuse publicly, gaslighting behavior is much more covert. Gaslighters know how to fly under the radar. They are adept at undermining an employee's self-esteem, confidence, and sense of reality in subtle, sneaky, and hard-to-prove ways. It's often your word against theirs, which makes going to other leaders or HR difficult."[10]

Preston Ni, an executive coach who writes about how to communicate effectively and handle difficult people, shares a few specific traits of gaslighting that differentiate it from normal workplace challenges:

- **Pervasive negative gossip** about your performance, credibility, or personality, creating a cultural narrative with no supporting evidence.
- **A public smear campaign** where you are denigrated in meetings; performance evaluations; customer and client reviews. These comments are based on falsehoods, a smear campaign designed to damage your reputation and credibility.
- **Ongoing professional exclusion.** This might show up as the "Good Ol' Boys Club," the glass ceiling, or other kinds of in-group bias where you are repeatedly excluded

from networking, development, leadership, and other vital career opportunities.

- **Inequitable treatment.** Perhaps you are a person of color being treated differently than your white colleagues, or you're a woman watching your male colleagues advance more quickly. A recent study at MIT showed female employees are still less likely to be promoted than their male counterparts, despite outperforming them and being less likely to quit.[11] And yet, if you try to confront the powers that be, you get told you're "too sensitive" or to "stop playing the feminist card."

- **Evasion and denial.** When you approach the gaslighter, they deny everything. They're defensive, dismissive, or evasive. When you try to clearly present the facts, they escalate things, either becoming overtly aggressive or defaulting to passive-aggressive behaviors that ooze into every subsequent interaction.[12]

Notice a throughline? The number one sign of gaslighting is that the behavior is persistent: it continues over a period of time.[13] You start to ask yourself, *Am I making this up?* Or you rationalize it away: *He probably didn't mean it like that. I'm reading too much into things.* Or you cling to an old narrative: *It was such a supportive environment when I started. I must be exaggerating.*

Environments are fluid. They can—and do—change. People you've always had good relationships with might start behaving differently as you climb the ranks. Your colleagues and bosses are human, too. They've got their own histories, and may feel competitive or threatened as you advance. We've talked about Tall Poppy Syndrome, when successful leaders are "resented, disliked or criticized due to their successes."[14] If you are caught up in this syndrome, you may sense a marked tonal shift. But if you're the only one noticing, you'll be right back where you started: hearing monsters in the attic that no one else seems to notice.

Unfortunately, most of us have found ourselves in an environment that permits, if not promotes, gaslighting. Too many organizations keep gaslighters on the payroll; they're often high up in the ranks. Sometimes, this can be addressed and ameliorated. Other times, it can't.

The key to identifying—and ultimately confronting—gaslighting is to take note of repeated patterns over time. The same is true for a fear-based culture. Those dead bodies in the boardroom aren't a one-time occur-

Pattern recognition is one of the most essential skills you'll need as you step into leadership roles.

rence; they continue to pile up. A hyper-competitive environment works the same way. You see your colleague repeatedly undercut and undermine others to get ahead.

Pattern recognition is one of the most essential skills you'll need as you step into leadership roles. Once you learn to recognize those patterns, you can take the necessary steps to break them. You now have more power and authority to change culture—but you have to be smart about it. That's where strategy comes into play.

Protect Yourself First

It probably won't surprise you to learn that a strategic approach to an unhealthy environment doesn't start with the environment at all. It starts with you.

The more you can respond from a centered and calm place, the more you'll be able to clearly and objectively understand your environment. Then, when someone says or does something that doesn't land right, you'll know it's not appropriate instead of questioning your reaction to it. Remember those lessons from Chapter 4: You would never allow someone to talk to your daughter or best friend that way—and you would never say or do that to someone else. Why? Because you wouldn't want to instill fear or make them doubt themselves.

I suggest every leader take three smart, strategic steps when navigating a toxic environment:

1. Recognize Reality

Facing your own denial is not easy. When you're in a toxic environment, clarity is next to impossible. But you need clarity in order to be honest with yourself. Only then can you get a bead on what's really happening. When your intuition is throwing up red flags and your body is sending warning signals, don't ignore them. You must acknowledge it internally before you can move forward.

Once you've done that, evaluate your situation objectively. How are you being treated? Do you feel safe and supported by the people around you? Or do you dread going to work every day? If it's the latter, acknowledge that how you're feeling is real. Also remember that you may need emotional backup to handle the situation effectively—which takes us to the second step.

2. Gather Support

Hopefully, by now, you've built relationships with trusted peers at your organization who can affirm your reality. If you're in a toxic environment, chances are they're suffering, too, making them ideal sounding boards. Lean on these trusted colleagues. Ask them for their honest appraisal and assessment of the situation. Are they perceiving things the way you are? Connecting with people you trust and asking for their input is a great way to figure out what's happening.

Now is the time to mobilize your support network. Often, when I share a story from work with my network, my peers can see it in a way I can't. As objective third parties, they have an outside perspective—and a clarity I don't. If you don't have a strong support network, I'll tell you how to cultivate one in Chapter 9.

Once you have confirmed you're in a toxic environment, it's time for step three.

3. Make Your Move

Here's where you figure out the right course of action. It requires preparation, clarity, and courage.

First, document the specifics: dates, promises made, work completed, and outcomes achieved. For example Rena, who was told she'd take on a leadership role, might prepare by:

- Listing specific dates when promises were made about the role
- Compiling examples of responsibilities she's already handling
- Gathering any evidence of positive feedback or performance outcomes
- Researching industry standards for compensation in similar roles

Next, request a formal meeting rather than an impromptu conversation. Say something like, "I'd like to schedule time to discuss my role and future with the company. Would Tuesday at 2 p.m. work?"

When you meet, use clear, factual statements: "I've been performing the responsibilities of Senior Manager for two years now. This includes [specific examples]. Yet my title remains Associate Manager, my compensation is at the previous level, and I haven't been added to the governance committees typically attended by people in this role. I'd like to understand the timeline for aligning my title, compensation, and inclusion with the work I'm already doing."

That conversation will reveal a lot. Pay attention not just to what they say but to body language and tone. Are they defensive, dismissive, or engaged? You'll quickly learn if they're going to back you or not.

If they deny making promises or minimize your contributions, you may be experiencing gaslighting. Respond calmly with something like, "I understand we have different recollections. I'd like to focus on finding a path forward based on my demonstrated contributions."

If they promise change, establish concrete next steps before ending the meeting. "So to confirm, by next Friday you'll provide a written offer with the new title and compensation package, correct?"

Before you take action, set realistic expectations. Toxic leaders rarely respond well to feedback. When confronted, they may retaliate in subtle ways. Since these behaviors can be hard to prove, escalating to upper leadership or HR requires careful documentation.

If you do choose to confront them, focus on solutions rather than blame. As we'll explore further in Chapter 9, building a personal board of directors is crucial for navigating these challenging situations. Having advisors who serve as mirrors for you can help you rehearse difficult conversations, provide objective perspectives, and support you through the process makes all the difference in maintaining your confidence and clarity.

Once you've addressed the situation, watch closely for what happens next. If you're seeing significant changes in a positive direction, fantastic! By opening an honest dialogue, you've made it a healthier environment for everyone.

If it becomes apparent that this isn't resolvable—or if they start treating you worse and you're miserable going to work—you have the power to walk away.

The Mirror Effect Workbook & *Journal* includes exercises to help you objectively assess your environment, identify early warning signs of toxicity, and develop strategies for responding effectively. These reflections support you in recognizing patterns of fear-based, competitive, or gaslighting behaviors before they undermine your confidence and well-being.

Safeguard Your Well-Being

Navigating toxic environments demands vigilance not just in your professional actions, but in safeguarding your mental and physical health. Consider establishing firm boundaries between work and personal life—perhaps by creating transition rituals when you leave the office, or maintain a separate phone for work communications that you can put away during personal time.

Track your energy levels and stress responses systematically. Notice when certain interactions consistently drain you and document specific patterns. This creates objective distance from emotional situations and provides valuable data about your experience.

Build resilience through external anchors—structured activities outside work that keep you grounded in your identity beyond your professional role. Whether it's community service, creative pursuits, or physical challenges, these anchors remind you of your multidimensional worth.

Consider professional support from someone with expertise in workplace dynamics—not just for emotional processing, but for strategic perspective. This might be a career coach, a therapist specializing in professional environments, or a trusted mentor who's navigated similar waters.

Remember that preserving your well-being during difficult workplace situations isn't self-indulgence; it's ensuring you maintain the mental clarity, emotional stability, and physical energy required to make sound decisions about your future. Your long-term success depends on your ability to weather these challenges without permanent damage to your confidence, judgment, or health.

Step into Your Power

Navigating difficult work environments can be demoralizing and draining. If you're doing it right now, take these steps to keep yourself afloat until you can change your situation.

- **Embrace your inner strength.** Remember, you're already powerful beyond measure. Pair that with the fact that no one can define your worth without your consent, and you're well on your way to achieving things you never thought possible.
- **Do the work.** Continue the internal work of confronting fears, dismantling limiting beliefs, and cultivating self-compassion to connect with your authentic self.
- **Pay attention to your surroundings and see the shift as you level up.** Recognize that while you may not control your work environment, you can control your reactions and behaviors. Further, acknowledge the reality that dynamics change as you ascend to leadership roles, especially when you're dealing with sophisticated individuals in executive positions.
- **Manage challenging personalities.** When you feel the push and pull of challenging personalities, you may feel compelled to either react to everything around you or conform to toxic surroundings. Understand the importance of getting centered and thoughtful—even in uncomfortable situations. But that doesn't mean you have to accept bad behavior. You can always decide that it's time to walk away.

- **Identify toxic environments.** Learn to recognize three common toxic environments at the highest organizational levels: fear-based workplaces, cutthroat competitive cultures, and gaslighting environments. And, importantly, know what you can do to foster psychological safety to cultivate innovation and positive outcomes.
- **Protect yourself first when you find yourself in toxic situations.** Recognize reality by acknowledging your feelings and seeking clarity about your environment. Gather support from trusted peers who can provide different perspectives and validate your experiences. Make your move strategically through direct conversations, realistic expectations, and firm boundaries when addressing problematic behaviors.
- **Prioritize your well-being above all else.** Your success depends on maintaining your mental clarity, emotional stability, and physical energy. Establish boundaries between work and personal life, track your responses to workplace stressors, build resilience through activities outside work, and don't hesitate to walk away when a situation proves unsalvageable.

Take this advice to heart and, in the words of Beyoncé, you'll be "flying over bullshit." (I love that line.) You're not on the ground, muscling your way through a miserable situation. You're flying so high above it nothing can take you down.

And that's a skill that will also serve you well in dealing with our next subject: egotists, assholes, and bad actors.

CHAPTER 6

TYRANTS AND RIVALS AND DECEIVERS (OH MY!)
Working with Wounded People

"You can't control how other people receive your energy. Anything you do or say gets filtered through the lens of whatever personal stuff they are dealing with at the moment."

–Mel Robbins

A t a happy hour with a group of CEOs, one of the most seasoned members of the group—a talented executive who's run multiple companies—pulled me aside. "Can I ask you a question?" she said. "What do you think about so-and-so?"

What she was really asking was, "Is it just me who has concerns about this person?" Like so many women leaders, she was wondering if the warped reflection this person showed her—one of inadequacy and doubt—was actually true. Difficult people often act like distorted mirrors, reflecting back versions of ourselves that make us question our competence, our worth, and our right to be in the room.

So-and-so, who will remain anonymous, is a well-respected and much-beloved senior leader in our community. People love this man. He's your classic white, sixty-something senior executive who commands a lot of respect. He's also capable of acting badly, especially toward women.

So what did I say to my fellow female CEO when she asked what I thought of this man?

"It's not you," I said. "Trust me."

She immediately relaxed. And then she opened up about her experience. When they'd worked together, he hadn't supported her. She felt like she couldn't do anything right around him. She stopped trusting herself and doubted her every move.

I assured her this was not her problem; it was very clearly his. The same thing had happened to multiple other women we knew, as well as some men. This guy would pretend to be supportive, and then a day later, he'd be at a meeting, claiming, "I didn't say that. I didn't agree to that." He was known to cause the people around him to doubt themselves.

The woman I was speaking with told me she'd had panic attacks. At the worst of it—when he was yelling at her every day—she couldn't sleep. Eventually, she left for a high-level position at a new company. Almost a year later, she is thriving. When I reminded her she never has to work with him again, tears sprang to her eyes.

This story highlights something I've observed repeatedly throughout my career: The people who cause the most damage in professional environments often aren't the obvious Tyrants. They're the sophisticated manipulators who present one face while operating with another, leaving their targets questioning their own reality and worth.

A Whole Other Type

We typically think of assholes as a certain type. They're bullies—loud, obnoxious, mean. They don't get along with people. They're dismissive and disruptive. In some ways, this kind of asshole is relatively easy to deal with. At least they're not trying to hide who they are.

But at the highest levels of an organization, there's a whole other type of asshole. They are sophisticated and cunning. They've risen to those levels because of their people skills. They are masterful at cultivating relationships, manipulating people, and influencing situations. I had no idea these kinds of assholes existed until I reached those levels myself.

If you are in a leadership position where you get to choose the people you hire and work with, great. You may impose the "No Asshole Rule," which is as simple as it sounds: You don't work with assholes. Period. Instead, you choose to consciously surround yourself with people who share your values. Individuals who are honest, fair, and unafraid to have upfront conversations.

Having said that, you're also in the business world. When you take on a new position or join a new company, the assholes may have been previously installed. Many leaders do not have a choice about the people they work with. You may be surrounded by some real jerks with a lot of money and power. You may have to work with assholes, at least for a while, to achieve your goals. It's not always easy to stay true to yourself while doing so, but you don't have to forfeit your authenticity. The secret is to develop a unique skill set, one you may not have needed before.

These powerful people don't think like us. They don't act like us. Here's what you need to learn to set yourself up for success with them.

Playing the People Game

I recently had a conversation with a senior executive at a successful fintech company. She was having real struggles at the board level, and when she brought it up to one of the other women on the board, her colleague said, "You have to understand what's really going on. What are people saying to you, what are people not saying to you, and are you reading between the lines?"

When we step into leadership roles, we're in a whole new league. We are surrounded by different types of individuals from vastly different backgrounds. We often assume the best, sure that our new colleagues operate with the same values and principles that we do. Unfortunately, that's not always the case.

It dawned on my friend that this woman was right: She'd been trying to reconcile two different sets of rules. Because she was unaware that the board was not playing by the same ones, she'd missed her chance to be proactive. She had not lined up other board members to be on her side—she hadn't made allies—and was not in control of the situation. Ultimately, she was playing a *different game*.

In these high-stakes environments, you must learn to read the people with whom you work. Understand who they are, what motivates them, and what's important to them. They may say one thing and do another—which is why you must pay close attention to not only what is said, but what is *not* said. That also means interrogating *why* they act the way they do. Remember: they're human, too. (More details on how to do all this later in the chapter.)

The thing is that you must do all of that from a calm, centered place. Easier said than done, right? But it's the only way to play the game while staying true to your values. Once you've found your center, you'll realize their behavior is about them, not you. They may be a powerful opponent in the game, but your power is rooted in your authentic self. That's always a win.

This is why it's critical to do the inner work first. You have to know yourself before you can deal with anyone else. We've talked about practicing self-compassion as you face the fear, insecurity, doubt, and shame so many of us carry. When you're coming from a grounded place, it becomes a lot easier to show more compassion to others—even the assholes.

As my own spiritual journey has evolved, I've come to understand that we are all suffering, and we are all wounded. When you meet someone who doesn't seem caring or compassionate toward others, you have to wonder: How are they treating themselves? Genuine compassion starts inside our own hearts before it can spill outward. Sometimes assholes are simply insecure humans who haven't done the inner work.

I've learned to get curious and ask questions. Who are these people? What makes them tick? How are they acting in ways that satisfy their needs, wants, and desires? How can I influence this situation to the best of my ability? How do I work *with* them to get done what I need to get done?

The more I claim my power, the more I realize I can deal with anyone. It's a lot less personal. I have no enemies. I'm not going to tolerate bad behavior toward others, and if someone is truly unethical, I never compromise my integrity. If I'm being abused or see someone else being abused, I walk away. But until a situation gets to that point, I try to suspend judgment to better understand the people around me, leading from a place of compassion.

It may seem counterintuitive that **the strongest defense against ego, power, and greed is compassion.** But it's a powerful play in the playbook. When I turn my compassion outward, something shifts. I've learned to be a lot more forgiving. Everyone is dealing with their own issues the best they can—even the assholes. *Especially* them. On the outside, they may seem like Tyrants, Rivals, and Deceivers. But there's often more to the story. The better you understand how they play the game, the better equipped you are to play it on *your* terms. With that in mind, let's talk about who you may run into in the hallowed halls at the top of an organization.

> **The strongest defense against ego, power, and greed is compassion.**

The Tyrant

Tyrants are masters of their domain. These are smart, talented individuals who've worked hard to get where they are. They have dazzling résumés. They're used to being the ones in control; that's the way they like it. A Tyrant will often think their way is the best way to do something, and they don't take kindly to being told otherwise.

Tyrants are bullies cut from more sophisticated cloth. But sometimes they're just as loud and disrespectful as the playground bullies we knew as kids. I once sat on a board of a successful biotech company with a bunch of gray-haired white men and one white woman. I was, per usual, the only woman of color. The male board members weren't all Tyrants, but there was one who fit the bill.

During a particularly memorable board meeting, he started yelling at me, saying my suggestions were ridiculous and that I couldn't possibly draw conclusions from the clinical drug trial with the amount of data that was currently available. I'm a clinical drug developer, mind you. This man has never developed a drug in his life.

Things could have gotten nasty. I could have yelled back at him or undermined his lack of expertise by trumpeting mine. But I knew that wasn't the right tack. Not for a Tyrant, someone who enjoys sitting on his throne, who might get hostile if he senses someone trying to usurp him. I knew he'd never listen if I chose that path.

Instead, I grounded myself. I didn't raise my voice or come out swinging. I calmly said, "I agree with you. However, because we have early data on ten patients, there are things you need to start thinking about and preparing for now." I explained where I was coming from, that I knew we'd need several months for the next phase of development, and in the meantime, we could start thinking about this from a biological perspective, considering what might be going on and how we could address it proactively. "That's what I would do in your shoes," I finished.

The Tyrant actually listened. I had gently and respectfully made my case, drawing on my considerable experience—and he listened. I didn't have to shame him or question his authority; I just had to share mine.

I was able to do this because I recognized that his harsh reflection was not an accurate mirror of my abilities. Tyrants often project their own insecurities onto others, creating warped reflections that make us doubt ourselves. But when we understand that the distortion comes from their lens—not our reality—we can stand firm in our expertise and worth.

Consequently, I got what I wanted. It was clear to everyone that I definitely belonged at that table. I reaffirmed my expertise and achieved an outcome that served all of us. In other words, I played the game without ever sacrificing my values or authentic self.

A few years earlier, I would have been jarred by him yelling and disrespecting me in front of the board. Not anymore. I treated him with compassion because I understood what was at the core of his response: He was scared.

This man had made a huge investment in the company, and he didn't want to make the mistake of over-interpreting the data. A perfectly reasonable concern. Because I didn't take his rant personally, I could see it was about his fear and exposure. He didn't want to be wrong, but not just because he was an asshole. He didn't want to be wrong because there could be grave consequences—for his patients, his shareholders, his job, his family.

Here's what Tyrants won't tell you: They often have a deep-seated fear of being seen as vulnerable, since they equate vulnerability with a loss of power.[1] They may inadvertently create in-groups where they can wield that power without being questioned. This can create an exclusive out-group populated by anyone who doesn't fall in line or appears to be "different." This means that, whether intentionally or not, many Tyrants will sideline people of color, LGBTQ+ professionals, disabled employees, and, of course, women.[2]

For example, research out of Duke University has shown that some male Tyrants view women's inclusion as a threat to their masculinity: "Men don't discriminate against women because they view women as less qualified but rather because they are trying to protect the social power men hold through membership in the 'boys' club.'"[3] When you understand that so much of their behavior arises out of fear, you can address those fears directly.

Ask Why

No one loves working with a Tyrant. At best, they're over-critical and frustrating. At worst, they make others feel afraid. When I encounter a Tyrant in the workplace, I ask myself: *Why* are they acting this way? Sometimes that question yields answers I don't expect.

As I've climbed the ladder, I've come to understand we're all doing our best to survive—while also being driven by our FIDS. For many women and disenfranchised leaders, that can come out as the four arche-types we discussed: the People-pleaser, the Imposter, the Bitch Boss, and the Micromanager. For men and other people in positions of power, it can come out as anger, greed, and a need for control. Their refusal to relinquish power is one of their coping mechanisms, a habit so deeply ingrained they may not even be aware of it.

Sometimes being a Tyrant is a way to cope with deeper inner issues. Maybe they survived an abusive childhood where they had their power stripped away. Maybe they've lived in fear most of their lives and don't know how to create any other kind of environment. Maybe they watched people they love struggle with addiction or substance abuse, making them terrified of losing control.

Does this excuse their bad behavior? Nope. If someone talks down to me or uses a certain tone, I see it as a red flag. But I don't take it per-sonally. My first response is to show compassion and give the Tyrant a little grace. Responding from that centered place helps *me* see the whole picture, empowering me to make healthy decisions about what's accept-able and what's not.

I try to stay as objective as possible. For me, that means taking a moment to analyze the way someone is acting and what's truly moti-vating their behavior. This helps me better understand the collective group dynamic and how each individual exists inside it. It also pro-vides insight on how I can make an impact of my own. (More on that in Part III.)

The Rival

Previously, I referenced an EY/espnW global study that dug into the sports experience of women in senior management positions: 94 percent of women in the C-suite played sports, 52 percent at the university level.[4] Sports set us up to have insights into all kinds of games. Whether out on the field or inside the boardroom, there's always a playbook—and we have to learn that playbook if we want to compete.

I didn't grow up playing on sports teams, and my family certainly didn't encourage me to get out there and compete. As a young Indian girl, I was told to listen, serve, and not make any trouble. Consequently, I didn't learn how to be a good sport. When I started competing with people in my career—a dynamic that comes with the job—I had a very "it's you or me" mentality, because I thought I would be taken out. I was terrified I'd get permanently benched.

My daughter, on the other hand, is a total pro. She's played a lot of sports, and she's intensely competitive—but also incredibly kind. When she knocks down a player on the soccer field, I watch her reach down, pull them up, and say, "Great play." I'm amazed every time I see her smile and high-five her opponents at the end of the game, regardless of who wins or loses. It's a skill I never learned as a kid, and one I'm so glad she's developed. She operates in the world very similar to my son, who, from an early age, was able to compete with his friends academically and in athletics in a gracious and respectful manner.

There's a distinction between healthy competitors—the ones who high-five each other at the end of the game—and the ones who will do anything, no matter how damaging to themselves or others, to win. I call this personality type the Rival.

Rivals are capable, charming, and ambitious. They've had to be that way to earn their spot—or, at least, that's the narrative they have about themselves. Beneath the surface, Rivals often struggle with imposter syndrome. Studies have shown that imposter syndrome affects the highest-level competitors in sports and business.[5] Because these people don't feel like they truly deserve to be at the top, they are hyper aware that there are only so many roles or positions available, and they're desperate to not lose theirs.

If we can look through the same lens of compassion as we did with the Tyrant, we come back to a simple question: What has happened in these people's lives to make them feel like there's never enough to go around—and that *they* are not enough?

We all bring our own issues to the table, no matter how much we want to leave them behind. In my own experience, toxically competitive people are often dealing with deeply internalized shame. I know this because I *was* that person. Now I can recognize what truly motivates the Rival. Instead of feeling like I must be extra competitive to win, I feel great compassion for this person who's stuck on the hamster wheel, trying so hard to outrun their shame.

Once we see things from that perspective, a new narrative emerges. Many of us exist in workplace cultures that do not provide a level playing field, equal pay, or equal opportunities. It's enough of a challenge getting the job in the first place, no matter how much talent and experience we bring to the table. We've been the only one in the room so long, we've started to believe there can only be one of us; there isn't space for anyone else. This can turn us into ruthless Rivals when that's not who we want to be.[6]

Unfortunately, competitive women leaders are sometimes perceived as combative, even when we're not. As we've seen, we get accused of having "sharp elbows" or being Bitch Bosses. While our male colleagues are rarely challenged for their ambitions, ambitious women are labeled as either overtly aggressive or passive-aggressive.

This double standard puts women in an impossible position. We're expected to compete in a business world that inherently values and rewards competition, yet we're penalized for displaying the very traits needed to succeed. Despite these contradictions, many of us find ways to embrace healthy competition on our own terms. I may not have grown up playing competitive sports like my daughter, but I've learned to function at my highest level as a leader by bringing my authentic competitive spirit to the table. When I succeed—when I metaphorically "score a goal"—it feels rewarding precisely because I've had to navigate these complex expectations. Most leaders, regardless of gender, enjoy the thrill of bringing their A-game; it's why we worked so hard to get here in the first place.

If we can meet people where they are, no one has to suffer alone. We recognize that we're all doing our best to survive and thrive in these high-stakes environments. We're all in the same boat, working through issues. And while we can't take accountability for anyone else's inner work, we can certainly engage fully and wholeheartedly in our own.

Are there people whose insatiable thirst to win makes them behave in toxic and harmful ways? Of course. I've worked with leaders like this, and I'm guessing you have, too. Just don't lose sight of the fact that everyone is fighting their own hard battles. If you see an opportunity to shift from competition to collaboration, seize it. Collaboration is one of my core values, so I try to model it in everything I do. In a successful collaboration, we *all* win.

The Deceiver

Have you ever sensed a knot forming in the pit of your stomach during a conversation because you felt as if someone were pulling the wool over your eyes? Or stepped into a room—maybe a boardroom—where everyone stopped talking the moment you entered? Maybe the hair on the nape of your neck stood up, because you knew, you just *knew* they were talking about you.

These physical responses are our bodies reading the energy around us and waving a red flag. Sometimes our bodies respond more quickly than our brains. For those of us who've spent our whole lives pretending things are okay when they're not, our bodies may speak the language of intuition while our conscious minds struggle to catch up.

Sometimes intuition is a powerful ally, especially when the people around us say one thing and do another. Our brains make us doubt ourselves, but our bodies say, *Something is wrong here.* We've talked about environments that aid and abet gaslighting. But what about the people who thrive inside those environments? The ones who try to negate your reality and tell you it's all in your head?

I call this personality type the Deceiver. These people are sophisticated and masterful "control artists" with a proven knack for manipulating situations. They surround themselves with acolytes who think they can do no wrong, and if you dare challenge them or speak out about an unhealthy environment, they deny there's a problem. They may even retaliate or enact punitive measures. Deceivers may also be Tyrants—there's plenty of overlap there—but they don't have to be. They can also be quiet disruptors, spreading noxious gossip or creating smear campaigns to take others down.

Great leadership and true power come from authenticity.

Once again, it's all about power. One of the most common reasons people gaslight is to gain power over others and get what they want.[7] It could be something small: a snide remark from a colleague or months of dismissive behavior during board meetings. Your mentor might advise you to not wear your heart on your sleeve … and then later, after following their advice, you discover they've been telling the rest of the company that you're a cold, hard bitch. Or like the example we saw in the last chapter, you were promised a role or promotion that never materialized. When you asked what happened, the board acted like you misunderstood, even though you have the emails that say otherwise.

When you are being gaslit like this, you're trying to reconcile two realities: the one you're inhabiting, and the one you're being *told* you're inhabiting. Deceivers are perhaps the most dangerous type of warped mirror in the workplace. They deliberately show you a distorted reflection of yourself and your reality, making you question your own perceptions and memories. The cognitive dissonance you feel is the result of trying to reconcile what you know to be true with the false reflection they're presenting to you. Finding accurate mirrors—trusted colleagues and mentors who reflect your true capabilities and experiences—becomes essential when dealing with these types of leaders.

Cognitive dissonance reveals a kind of incongruence. The way you're being treated in your environment misaligns with who you know yourself to be. Since your interactions are colored by fear, you interact with others differently than you want to. You don't feel like your authentic self.

Great leadership and true power come from authenticity. If you don't have that, you won't have power or influence over the people you lead. But if you're being gaslit, you must first and foremost have compassion for yourself. What's happening isn't your fault. You deserve better.

You may not be in a position where you can walk away from a toxic environment—or you may choose not to do so. At least not yet. Just remember the three steps from the last chapter: Recognize Reality, Gather Support, and Make Your Move. And trust your intuition as you figure out what's really going on. It will guide you down the right path.

Step into Your Power

You can start by embodying the "No Asshole Rule" whenever you can. If you're in a leadership position where you get a say in who you bring on board or work with, fantastic! Why not build a healthy, supportive environment where people share your values? But if you don't have that kind of power—or if you inherit an existing asshole when you step into a new role—it might be time to:

- **Get curious about Tyrants, Rivals, and Deceivers.** Ask the right questions. How were these people shaped by their backgrounds? Why do they act the way they do? Engage with them from a centered place and try to exercise compassion. If things can shift, great. If not, assess the situation and do what's right for you.
- **Address the why.** Once you understand *why* a Tyrant, Rival, or Deceiver has taken on that role, attempt to address the concern behind the facade. For example, if it seems that fear is the cause of a leader's behavior, you

can do your best to assuage their concerns and find a solution that's beneficial for all.

- **Tell yourself, "It's them, not me."** We all have baggage—it's part of being human. But that doesn't mean you have to pick up other people's bags. When you're working with people who exhibit toxic behavior, remind yourself that it's not about you—even if that means literally saying it out loud. That can make it easier to collaborate and get things done.

It's not on you to change anyone else's behavior. But if you treat others with understanding and compassion, you can find ways to work alongside leaders you find challenging. Remember: Difficult people are wounded people. When you stand your ground and lead with your values, these relationships might even blossom in surprising ways.

When you know your values, you are better equipped to create alliances with those who share your vision.

Further, **when you know your values, you are better equipped to create alliances with those who share your vision.** You nurture an environment of collaboration and respect. You create the kind of place that makes people *want* to go to work every day. A place where both you and your colleagues flourish.

It's important to note, though, that every working environment is a two-way street. It's not just about how those you encounter show up; it's also about how *they* perceive *you*.

CHAPTER 7

THE GIFT OF MISPERCEPTION

Assessing and Addressing the Ways You're Perceived

"Don't think about making women fit the world—think about making the world fit women."

–Gloria Steinem

aya will never forget the day her boss said, "I'm scared of you."

She was in her first role at a well-respected law firm. Maya tried hard to prove herself to her new colleagues, hoping to establish herself as a partner. As a result, she worked all the time, desperate to please the senior law partners and be a team player—and insecure about whether or not she was succeeding. She was often the only woman in the room, trying her best to fit in, even though her interests were very different from her male peers and superiors.

Maya had studied law, earning her JD at Harvard after earning an MBA at Wharton and spending a short stint at a prestigious consulting firm. Her time at the consulting firm gave her an interesting perspective on law and prompted the additional degree. By the time she joined the law firm, she understood the importance of hitting targets and achieving business objectives. She also had a heart for justice and was committed to championing the law firm's clients. And to date, she felt she had done just that: worked hard to advance the firm's objectives, all while being a respectful and collaborative member of the team.

So when her boss confessed he was scared of her, she was floored.

What about Maya was scary? Was it that she was a young woman of color who didn't look like everyone else at the firm? Were there things she was doing that made people uncomfortable, even when she was trying so hard to fit in? Though she was familiar with unconscious and conscious bias, she didn't understand the nuances and intricacies of how biases worked, nor did she want to call attention to herself by complaining. So she kept her head down and tried to do her best.

Maya's colleagues weren't bad people. She actually liked her boss. Surely they could see all the excitement and expertise she brought to the table. Maybe, she reasoned, it had more to do with the fact that she'd come from a different kind of work environment. At the consulting firm, she was encouraged to speak up if something wasn't right. Dissenting opinions were par for the course. At the law firm, it seemed she and her peers were expected to keep their mouths shut and defer to their superiors. No one said so directly, but she could sense it in the culture: an unspoken understanding that opinionated associates were aggressive and selfish.

As she sat with her boss's words, she replayed the months leading up to his admission. Shortly after being hired, she noticed her peers seemed to be favored by the partners. She didn't fully acknowledge it, though—not even to herself—because soon she was thrust into a major life change: She was pregnant with her first child.

Only when Maya came back from maternity leave did she see clearly how the dynamics had shifted. The environment felt uber-competitive—even more so than she was used to. It was as if she and her peers were being pitted against one another to see who would make it out alive. Plus, in her absence, she had been taken off the cases she was working on and reassigned those with a lower priority. That led to a conversation with her boss in which she asked him candidly what had changed.

For the first time since starting the job, Maya got emotional. She had always kept her walls up. She had to be professional, together, organized, and presentable at all times. But now she let her guard down, as did her boss. Finally, they were able to have a human-to-human conversation.

That's when he said, "I'm scared of you."

Maya's boss told her she was talented, but admitted he was uncomfortable with her because they didn't share the same background. This was a white male, thirty years her senior, no kids. She was his opposite in so many ways.

Her boss told her it wasn't just him who felt this way; many of her colleagues saw Maya as overly competitive. They were concerned that she was acting in her own interest, not for the good of the firm.

When Maya let her guard down and spoke her truth, her boss realized he'd misunderstood her. He then became softer, and recommended they spend more time together. He also advised her to spend more time with her peers and other law partners and let them get to know her.

But she still walked away feeling unmoored. She desperately wanted the team to feel her passion, to validate her blend of expertise in business and law. And she had tried so hard to belong.

Maya was facing an unpleasant truth: She hadn't been aware of how she was being perceived. Other people's perceptions of who she was did not sync up with the way she perceived herself. As a result, she was ostracized and sidelined. After she followed her boss's advice and spent time and energy developing better relationships with her partners, the firm's leadership openly acknowledged that they had misjudged her intentions. However, with her career still stalled, she gracefully planned her exit.

Maya's experience is not unusual. As a leader, you may face misperceptions that are patently untrue, grounded in conscious or unconscious bias and persistent stereotypes. They may alter your reflection, like a warped mirror. Sometimes, the perceptions people have about you will have kernels of truth but be rooted in a larger context and years of cultural conditioning that need to be acknowledged before the kernel can be addressed. At other times, others' perceptions will be true and hard to hear—yet they present an opportunity for growth. While it may sound difficult, if you approach others' perceptions with openness and humility, all of them can be gifts.

In this chapter, we'll talk about how to acknowledge, assess, and address these scenarios. Per usual, the work starts internally as you begin to cultivate more awareness around how you are perceived. Once you learn to navigate others' perceptions from a calm and centered place, you'll be able to move forward, setting yourself up for success without surrendering your power.

Who Does She Think She Is?

When we begin to investigate how, why, and when marginalized leaders are misperceived, it doesn't take long to suss out one key ingredient: bias.

Every disenfranchised professional is familiar with bias. Especially unconscious or implicit bias: the automatic and unintentional attitudes, assumptions, stereotypes, and prejudices that influence our decisions and actions.[1] These unconscious beliefs are dangerous because they are learned slowly over time, and we're not even aware of them.[2] They can actively reinforce stereotypes and lead to negative behavior ranging from subtle slights and snubs to toxic cliques, discrimination, harassment, and even hate.[3]

Unconscious bias is present all around us and notoriously hard to combat since it exists outside of conscious thought. "Implicit bias is like the smog that hangs over a community," says journalist Shankar Vedantam, host and creator of the *Hidden Brain* podcast. "It becomes the air people breathe."[4]

There are many kinds of unconscious biases, and they can—and do—coexist. As a woman of color, I've experienced gender and racial bias. As a member of the Indian community, I've experienced cultural bias. When I was just starting out in biotech, I faced age bias as a young woman. Truthfully, I still do face all these biases, but I am much better equipped to identify and deal with them.

I've also experienced kinds of bias that don't get talked about as much. Conformity bias happens when we feel pressured to fit into a certain group or professional environment. This bias was certainly at play for Maya, who felt like she couldn't voice her honest opinion at work. She was also affected by affinity bias: when people favor others who share similar interests, backgrounds, and experiences. For her boss, this bias bridged the gap between unconscious and conscious: He openly acknowledged that he didn't feel comfortable around her, though he didn't go so far as to say it was because of her gender or race.

Acknowledging Affinity Bias

I want to stress that having biases does not make people inherently bad or evil. Take affinity bias as an example. As humans, our brains are actually wired for affinity bias. We have a psychological inclination to seek familiarity and comfort because back when we all lived in tribes, we had to bond deeply with people who looked and behaved like us in order to survive.[5] But in today's world, things have evolved quickly, and our brains haven't always kept up. Affinity bias becomes problematic when we don't pause to acknowledge and unpack the subtle ways in which we treat others differently if they don't look, speak, or act like us. In professional contexts, this can unconsciously dictate—and limit—the people we hire and work with.[6]

Affinity bias is just one of many unconscious biases that affect our perceptions and decisions in the workplace. These biases arise from deeply ingrained stereotypes and cultural messaging that we absorb throughout our lives. While affinity bias relates to our tendency to gravitate toward people like ourselves, other forms of bias directly impact how we perceive people from different backgrounds. These stereotypes create harmful shortcuts in our thinking that reduce complex individuals to simplistic caricatures based on their identities. Despite increased awareness and training in many organizations, these unconscious biases continue to shape workplace dynamics in profound ways. Their subtlety makes them particularly challenging to address, as they often operate below the threshold of our conscious awareness.

According to the Kirwan Institute for the Study of Race and Ethnicity, "These biases, which encompass both favorable and unfavorable assessments, are activated involuntarily and without an individual's awareness or intentional control.[7]" When a person of color is in a leadership role, their colleagues may make all sorts of assumptions based on the color of their skin. Many of these will be familiar: Black women are angry.[8] Latinx employees are lazy.[9] All Asians are intelligent and good at math.[10] South Asian women, like me, are submissive and hard-working. And it doesn't end there; biases extend to sexual orientation, religion, age, ability, body size, neurotypicality, among many others.

Uncovering Implicit and Explicit Bias

Some fascinating studies have been done on name bias, a corollary of racial bias. In 2003, economics professors at Chicago's Graduate School of Business and MIT conducted a landmark study: They sent out 5,000 fake resumes for 1,300 job openings, using both traditionally white-sounding names and distinctively Black-sounding names. The results were disturbing: Applicants with white-sounding names were 50 percent more likely to be contacted for job interviews.[11]

Twenty years later, economists from the University of California, Berkeley, and the University of Chicago set out to test whether the situation had improved. They sent 83,000 job applications to 108 Fortune 500 employers. The applicants all had similar experience, but half had names like Emily and Greg, the other half names like Jamal and Lakisha. The outcome was better than in the original study, but applicants with Black-sounding names were still called back 10 percent fewer times across the board. Even less at a handful of specific companies.[12] Unconscious, or implicit, bias is one area in which the old axiom holds true: Actions speak louder than words. Many operate with deeply held biases without even realizing it.

Then, of course, there is the kind of bias that is conscious and overt. Conscious or explicit bias occurs when assumptions, attitudes, and beliefs are held by people who are perfectly cognizant of their attitudes toward anyone they perceive as different.[13] I was recently trying to help a distressed company that needed guidance. I signed into a video conference room and was instantly greeted by the faces of ten white men, all over the age of fifty. Which is to say a room that looked remarkably like most of the other rooms I'd walked into over the course of my career.

This time, though, the lead investor acknowledged his bias right off the bat. He told me, "Of course you can be involved, Sheila ... with male gray-haired leadership." With my best Beyoncé swagger, I told him I had enough gray hair, thank you very much!

Sadly, I am so accustomed to hearing some version of that sentiment—as well as far less appropriate sentiments—that his words hardly fazed me. I actually appreciated that he brought his feelings out into the open, as opposed to the many colleagues who were supposed to be supporting me and revealed themselves to be subversive and manipulative. Even if they didn't say it out loud, they had the exact same underlying belief: *Who does she think she is?*

The best response to both kinds of bias is to raise awareness about it, identify it, and address it. To be clear, many people are actively engaged in doing this work. Everyone from the UN to UNICEF and the World Bank are working toward eradicating bias. For example, many are especially focused on being more inclusive toward young women in tech, with the full knowledge that "digital technologies could lead to more economic and social inequalities unless women are empowered by having access to technology and acquiring the skills needed to benefit from it."[14,15,16]

Though it may not seem that way, many people in positions of power are actively working to confront their biases, including plenty of white men. These leaders are committed to addressing their misperceptions by doing their own inner work, then using their power and privilege to interrogate broken systems. They are allies in the truest sense of the word. And when *allies* share their perceptions of you, this feedback might transition out of misperceptions and into the second kind of perception, which we'll talk about next.

But What If It's Kinda True?

We should all be able to be our authentic selves without fear of being labeled or facing retribution.

In Chapter 3, we discussed archetypes. These can sometimes be empowering, but they can also be harmful, especially when people cast you in a role you never asked to play. This is where archetypes and perceptions intersect because often the archetype is not one that a leader has consciously chosen for themselves. It is linked to the way they're perceived by others.

As I mentioned in Chapter 3, the four most common archetypes I've seen in organizations are the People-pleaser, the Imposter, the Bitch Boss, and the Micromanager. In some ways, the first two are more internal: You may catch yourself trying to please people to an unhealthy degree, running yourself ragged to keep them happy. And the professionals who feel imposter syndrome are, in my experience, extremely talented and high-performing, yet they doubt their every move, secretly certain they don't deserve their success and will be exposed.

Now consider the latter two, Bitch Boss and Micromanager. These archetypes are typically imposed by other people: the ones who think you've got "sharp elbows," and the ones who think you're too controlling. It's not like any kid grows up with dreams of becoming a Bitch or a Micromanager! And it can be painful when the misperceptions of others cast you in these roles.

But if we take a moment to explore those misguided perceptions, is it possible there's an element of truth to them? **We should all be able to be our authentic selves without fear of being labeled or facing retribution.** Someone once told me, "One of my biggest challenges is that I am like a

THE GIFT OF MISPERCEPTION 129

man, and that intimidates people. I am strong, capable, and assertive in my opinions. I also get shit done and am more focused on strategy and execution than many of my male peers." That should be okay.

The Bitch Boss label is most commonly ascribed to women leaders, for obvious reasons. And as we've seen, terms like "sharp elbows" are rarely used for men. When you're labeled as a Bitch Boss, people perceive you as aggressive and domineering. But there's an important distinction to make here: What others call "aggression" may simply be assertiveness. When you're passionate about hitting quarterly targets or improving profit margins, that shouldn't be held against you. And if you're labeled as "domineering," consider that you may be exhibiting the exact same leadership traits as Jack Welch, Rupert Murdoch, and Steve Jobs—all known for their authoritarian approach, yet all widely considered dynamic, effective leaders.

Similarly, if you've been labeled a Micromanager, remember that your attention to detail and high standards—qualities that likely helped you succeed throughout your career—might be misinterpreted. Perhaps your thoroughness is being misconstrued as a lack of trust.

When facing these misperceptions, consider how society and workplace cultures have shaped both your behavior and how others perceive it. When you've spent your career working twice as hard for half the credit, it makes sense that you've developed certain traits to survive and succeed. You might have shed some of the people-pleasing behaviors that weren't serving you or become more assertive about your needs and boundaries.

People may perceive you a certain way, one that doesn't always cast you in a favorable light. Your instinct might be to fight against these labels, to dismiss them entirely as misperceptions. But if a particular label really gets under your skin, it could be worth examining—not because it's completely accurate, but because understanding why you're being perceived this way can help you navigate these situations more effectively.

The question then becomes: how do you step into your power by claiming your authentic leadership style without succumbing to the FIDS—fear, insecurity, doubt, and shame? We'll talk more about that later. But here's a sneak peek: If you can operate from a more grounded place, taking the time to understand how you're being perceived and the context and circumstances around that perception, you will be in a far better place to acknowledge and address it.

Which leads us to the third type of perception: the one that's true.

How Do I Accept What's True?

Some of the perceptions people have about you are going to be unexpected. They may be challenging, hard to hear … and true. I've certainly received valid feedback that really shook me. Most of the leaders I know walk away from those conversations feeling stunned and confused that they are coming off in a way so different from what they intended. Sometimes the *opposite* way from what they intended. And guess what?

That's okay.

Feedback can be hard. It's also necessary. To move forward professionally, you must learn how to accept constructive feedback, calmly and gracefully, as you continue to advance in your career. A good leader is not someone who never gets any negative feedback whatsoever. A good leader is someone who can humbly accept feedback and incorporate it into their authentic leadership style.

You may feel as if you've been misunderstood—and that may well be true. But if you can figure out how and where the disconnect happened, you'll be able to face it head-on. When people share with you that the "you" you're presenting doesn't accurately reflect the authentic you, they are actually giving you a gift: the gift of perception. Sometimes there's a genuine opportunity to grow and evolve. And sometimes those perceptions give you insight into whether or not this job at this organization is the right fit for you.

As you've probably figured out by now, the ways people perceive you do not always fall neatly into one of these three categories. Misperceptions can have grains of truth, and true perceptions may still be flawed. The lines blur easily, which can make it even more difficult to know what deserves your attention and what you can take out with the trash.

Here's a story that illustrates the multifaceted nature of misperceptions: Several years ago, Irma was leading a team at a big public company. She had a significant corporate goal to meet by year's end, so she started pulling out all the stops to achieve it. Irma was trying to do what was right for the team and the company, and she was excited about setting all of them up for success.

To do that, she had to start working closely with all of her team members. She posed a big question to the group: *What is beyond possible?* Her goal was to problem-solve through innovation and teamwork. That meant taking a creative approach that the company wasn't used to. People got upset. They complained to their managers. Irma got called out for pushing too hard. She was labeled as "selfish." According to the team, all she cared about was achieving her larger-than-life goal. Team members said she was micromanaging their work. They told company leadership that she was hyper-competitive and not a team player.

"I was shocked," Irma told me. "I felt like I'd been completely misunderstood. Everything I was trying to do was for the benefit of the team and the company. To be honest, I was dealing with a lot of people who were *not* doing that. I had to step in to get things done."

What's interesting about this story is that, thanks to Irma, the company did meet their big corporate goal. They achieved it just before the end of the fiscal year, and because of that, the entire company got a bonus payout. Her drive and commitment had boosted *everyone's* bottom line.

Irma adds, "This isn't a humble brag. I share my story with people because it's a testament to how complex and complicated perceptions can be. I just felt so confused. All the shame and imposter syndrome I'd struggled with my whole life started to surface because some of the feed-back did hit on my soft spots, the stuff I worried about most."

I've known Irma for years. She *is* competitive, but that doesn't make her selfish. She *does* push her teams hard, but that doesn't make her a Tyrant or Micromanager. What her colleagues saw as her being combative was accurate, insofar as she came to work every day fighting—but she was fighting *for them*. They just couldn't see it. And yes, she was shaking things up at the company, implementing more creative strategies than they'd had in the past. But that wasn't her trying to hog the limelight. Irma was trying to leverage her insights and talents to find solutions that worked.

With the benefit of hindsight, she sees the situation with more clarity. There were various biases at play, in large part because she was a queer Latinx woman. People were more inclined to react to her in certain ways, no matter how she actually behaved.

"Now I can see all the red flags I couldn't see back then," Irma says. "That company was toxic. The culture was so negative. The company leadership was always undermining us, especially employees of color. At best, we were misunderstood; at worst, we were accused of—and blamed for—things we hadn't done." Shortly after Irma led the company to their corporate goal, she made her exit, landing at a company that valued the unique gifts she brought to the table.

I've met and counseled so many leaders who've had similar experiences. It can be particularly confusing when other people's perceptions don't match up with *each other's*, making it next to impossible to parse the helpful feedback from the fake news. Not everyone at Irma's company thought she was self-serving. Before she left, one of her colleagues pulled her aside and said, "You are amazing, Ir. You've done so much for us. You're a rock star!"

So how do you know who to listen to? By listening to the most important voice first: your own. Even if perceptions come from an external place, you must take accountability for the way you're perceived and align feedback with your authentic self. Is it completely off base? Does it resonate? If it gets under your skin, is it because it's a massive misperception informed by insidious biases? Or is it because something about it rings true? Does it hint at things you want to work on? Are there ways to adjust your actions and behaviors so that your external expression is more aligned with your internal truth?

In *The Mirror Effect Workbook & Journal*, you'll find prompts designed to help you process feedback, distinguishing between bias-driven misperceptions and valuable insights for growth. These exercises guide you through examining how others see you and how to respond from a place of self-knowledge rather than reactivity.

Step into Your Power

How do you handle feedback with grace and discernment? Think about what you take in and what you put out there. Here are five strategies for managing feedback that I like to share with leaders:

1. **Be vulnerable.** We've talked about Brené Brown and the current cultural movement toward vulnerability. Being vulnerable can be great—under the right conditions. My caveat here is that vulnerability looks different for marginalized leaders than it does for members of the majority. In the words of author and behavioral scientist Dr. Carey Yazeed, "Experts like Brené Brown encourage us to be 'vulnerable' and lean into difficult situations, but the lived experiences and societal traumas of Black women differ

from those of white women."[17] In her research, Yazeed discovered a significant gap in Brown's work: race. "Although her research is marketed to everyone," Yazeed says, "it is limited when examining the lived experiences of minority women."[18] Of course, when you are working with allies and people you trust, vulnerability can be a powerful tool in your tool kit. If you can go into these conversations calm, centered, and courageous, vulnerability becomes a sign of strength, not weakness. In Maya's story, her vulnerability with her boss opened an honest dialogue in which she finally understood the biases she was up against in that environment. Only then was she able to see clearly what was happening—and make her exit.

2. **Ask for feedback.** We all need feedback to grow. In companies with top-down, hierarchical leadership, feedback can be, at best, one-sided; at worst, tyrannical. But in a healthy and supportive environment, you might have the opportunity to ask for a 360 review. This type of performance evaluation garners feedback from multiple people in the organization, including direct reports, team members, peers, mentors, managers, administrators—sometimes even customers. If a 360 is working the way it's supposed to, you will get honest insight and constructive feedback from all sides: a sterling opportunity to better understand how you are being perceived by a diverse set of people in different parts of the organization. The goal is to receive feedback with humility and openness, knowing that you will hear a variety of viewpoints that may not always reflect your authentic self. Some perceptions will be accurate; others will miss the mark.

3. **Stand strong.** When receiving feedback, it's good to keep in mind that there will always be dissenting opinions. You can't make everyone happy. If there are recurrent themes, it may be worth taking a closer look at them. But recurrent themes may also reveal people's unconscious biases coming to the fore. The more aware you can be of the various factors that influence feedback, the better positioned you'll be to take what's helpful and discard the rest. This will help you know when to compromise, and when to take no bullshit and stand strong.

4. **Inspire others.** We'll talk more about this later, but for now I'll say this: Whenever you have the opportunity to be a role model—even in toxic environments full of biases and bad behavior—take it. After maneuvering through years of being misperceived and perceived in ways I didn't want to be, I've been able to help other leaders who are shocked and destabilized by other people's perceptions. In companies founded on a culture of scarcity, especially for disenfranchised leaders, my hope is to create abundance for the people around me. I'm grateful to be in the position to be able to help others. Be the change you want to see.

5. **Choose your battles.** You can't win 'em all, so pick the ones you want to fight. Sometimes it's worth it to challenge people's misperceptions or ask for feedback so you can shift the way you are perceived. Sometimes, it isn't.

We've talked at length about reclaiming your power and authentic self. Nowhere is this more important than when you are navigating other people's perceptions, which may or not be grounded in truth. The solution is for you to stay grounded.

Compassion has been a big theme in this book. In Part I, we talked about viewing yourself through the lens of self-compassion as you confront your own reactivity, conditioning, and the pervasive FIDS. As we've talked about knowing your environment in Part II, the idea is to turn that lens outward, using it to effectively assess and address what's going on around you.

Does being compassionate mean you have to put up with Tyrants, Rivals, and Deceivers? No. But it does mean giving others the benefit of the doubt. Keep in mind they won't always do the same for you; a lot of people simply aren't capable of it. But that's their own baggage, and you're not responsible for it. You can only be accountable for yourself.

If you're in an environment that doesn't support you as you take these steps, it may be time to walk away. You deserve an environment that does empower you. A culture where you can align your leadership style with your authentic self and surround yourself with people who lift you up instead of tearing you down. A place where no one questions that you are powerful beyond measure, least of all you. And that environment does exist. Let's talk about it.

CHAPTER 8

WHEN YOU KNOW, YOU KNOW

Finding an Environment Where You Can Thrive

> **"When you get to a place where you understand that love and belonging, your worthiness, is a birthright and not something you have to earn, anything is possible."**
>
> *–Dr. Brené Brown*

Imani was a sought-after executive in corporate development who had worked her way up over two decades, demonstrating passion, tenacity, and talent for building teams. Like many leaders from historically marginalized backgrounds, her path wasn't easy. She encountered countless biases, was snubbed in meetings, and got passed over for promotions. The organizations she'd worked for definitely didn't have a "No Asshole Rule," and she was frequently criticized for challenging the status quo —especially by older colleagues who seemed uncomfortable with her presence.

But Imani knew her worth and could see beyond the bullshit. From her first role in business development, she envisioned running her own company with a clear vision of how to do it. Her goal was to build a thriving, supportive culture aligned with her values. And that's exactly what she did.

When Imani launched her company, she took the "No Asshole Rule" to heart, shaping the culture around a simple mantra: "No Egos, No

Jerks, No Politics." She defined her organization's core values as humility, collaboration, respect, productivity, and excellence. To foster this supportive environment, she assembled a team who were not only brilliant and high-performing but who aligned with these values.

During hiring, Imani carefully assessed candidates for warning signs and conducted thorough reference checks to ensure alignment with the company's values. Her philosophy became infectious, embedded in every part of the organization. She built her board with people who supported her vision, recruiting diverse professionals who were eager to escape other boards full of egos and politics. She even applied the same approach to clients, working only with those who embodied the values her team championed.

The results spoke for themselves. Imani's company surpassed all metrics in its first year, the culture thrived, and challenges were addressed with compassion and clarity. Team members felt safe to speak up when something wasn't working, and the organization evolved accordingly. Imani had created a truly supportive environment where people felt safe to be authentic, coming to work each day full of hope, energy, and joy.

This may sound like a fairy tale. I assure you it isn't. Imani is an inspiring friend and colleague, and it's been my pleasure to watch her company thrive. She has created a space where everyone gets to live up to their full potential. Over and over, she sets up herself and her team for success. A great working environment that garners exceptional business results is possible. You *can* work in a place this amazing. In fact, you deserve to.

Of course, not everyone is in a position to cultivate an awesome culture from scratch. But the tools Imani used to build her company can be applied to numerous situations. You can find supportive, psychologically safe environments with the potential to be even better. And as a leader, you have the capacity to co-create a healthy, supportive environment for your team; to champion a safe space where egos are set aside, jerks have no place, and politics are minimal, if not non-existent.

It all starts with your vision.

Be Visionary

Before we go any further, take a moment to reflect on the kind of world you want to inhabit—at work and otherwise. Oprah, in all her brilliance, has been encouraging us to live our best life for almost two decades, but few of us have stopped to think about what that really means. So let's do that now.

What does your best life look like? What would you create for yourself if you had the power to make it happen (which, by now, you know you do)?

This is a great time to think about your purpose—what gets you up in the morning? What causes do you want to advance? How can your interests, skills, and dedication help you do something that really matters to you?

Now, let's think bigger. What kind of world would you build for others? What could you innovate or accomplish if you had the buy-in of a community? You can look to some of the biggest companies out there for inspiration. Nike's vision is, "To do everything possible to expand human potential." Apple's is, "To make the best products on earth and to leave the world better than we found it." Disney's is simply, "To make people happy." All of them capture big-picture thinking about what the world could look like for others.

What could you do that's never been done before? Feats that once seemed impossible—putting people on the moon, linking far corners of the globe through technology, developing life-saving vaccines in record time—have been accomplished with the imagination and commitment of visionaries and the companies and communities inspired by their brilliance and passion. Why can't that next great visionary be you?

Now, put it on paper. Create a vision board that captures what you truly want for yourself and maybe even for all of us. The stuff that doesn't seem possible right now. After all, to be the change, you first have to visualize it.

Next, you've got to consider your values.

Ensure Your Values Have Value

In recent years, the term "core value" has become a corporate buzzword. Every company has them. The question is, do they actually live them out?

Organizational health expert Patrick Lencioni defines core values as "the deeply ingrained principles that guide all of a company's actions; they serve as its cultural cornerstones."[1] Lencioni also points out that, for many companies, core values become a hollow construct; they look good on a website, but in reality they're meaningless. He offers an example of the four impressive-sounding values of a large corporation—communication, respect, integrity, and excellence—before sharing the name of the company: Enron.

The only way to make your core values meaningful is to imbue them in everything you do. The way you show up at work and at home. Board meetings and PTA sessions, marketing projects and volunteer efforts, standups with your team and heart-to-hearts with your best friends. You shouldn't have to be different people in different parts of your life. We spend ninety thousand hours or one-third of our lives at work. Shouldn't that time feel in alignment with who we are and what matters to us?[2]

I've been fortunate to build many teams in biotech, and there are four values I always come back to as my guiding principles: **humility, collaboration, excellence, and respect.**

Humility is of the utmost importance to me as a leader. It's the underpinning of how I've approached every leadership role. A leader with humility understands that success is not a solitary achievement, but rather a result of collaborative efforts. They recognize that their own contributions are just one piece of a larger puzzle. Humility is about being open, curious, and willing to learn from others, embracing a growth mindset that constantly seeks improvement and innovative solutions.

As I've embarked on my spiritual journey in recent years, humility continues to hold a special place in my heart. I firmly believe our talents and abilities are gifts bestowed on us by a greater source, making us part of a grand cosmic tapestry. By recognizing this interconnectedness and appreciating the blessings we've received, we can cultivate an atmosphere of gratitude and humility. But it also can be simpler than that.

Humility implies a sense of acceptance and non-judgment. It creates a safe and open workplace where everyone's ideas are valued, and people feel empowered to share their thoughts without fear of ridicule. When humility becomes a core value in an organization, it paves the way for a culture that values collaboration, inclusivity, and a shared sense of purpose. In that kind of environment, we can accomplish more together.

Which brings us to my second core value: **collaboration**, the lifeblood of any successful team. Business is rife with complex challenges that require different kinds of thinking. No one can achieve greatness alone. Collaboration is about recognizing that it takes a collective effort to overcome obstacles and achieve breakthroughs. It's about valuing each team member's unique contributions and supporting one another.

And by the way, when diverse perspectives are welcomed and promoted, the organization succeeds, too. As I've mentioned, multiple studies have shown that diversity in the workplace is great for a company's bottom line.[3]

Time and again, I've witnessed collaborative teams comprising different skills and viewpoints achieve remarkable things. When people come together to work toward a common goal, magic happens. "We're in this together" is my favorite catchphrase. Those four words encapsulate the very essence of collaboration, a mindset that fosters a spirit of cooperation, mutual respect, and shared responsibility.

When I'm evaluating a new work environment or potential team members, I always have collaboration in mind. How do individuals interact with one another? Do they make each other feel welcome and valued? Do they create an atmosphere where opinions are genuinely heard and respected? Collaboration thrives in an environment that encourages different perspectives and empowers individuals to bring their unique strengths to the table.

Further, do they celebrate each other's accomplishments and do their best to set each other up for success? Rather than fostering competition, those efforts encourage teamwork. In turn, everyone is equipped to contribute toward something bigger than individual career aspirations; a vision that seems to exceed what's possible. And rather than feeling intimidated, they feel inspired. That's the potential of true collaboration.

Now, when we collectively incorporate **excellence** in all that we do, we will inevitably deliver meaningful results. Why?

We're committed to doing what is beyond possible. Striving for excellence means committing to the continuous pursuit of the highest standards and the best possible outcomes in every endeavor. To get there, we take accountability, tapping into our growth mindset to constantly improve and learn. That guides all our activities. We can absolutely be demanding of ourselves, each other, and our organizations, especially when we are setting each other up for success and beating our milestones together. This commitment fuels a culture of continuous improvement, encouraging us and our organizations to push beyond comfort zones and embrace challenges as opportunities for growth.

Excellence instills a sense of pride and accomplishment in us, motivating every member of our teams to bring their best to the table and inspiring others to do the same. That sentiment inevitably shows in our work. A commitment to excellence enhances the quality of products and services, builds trust with stakeholders, and distinguishes an entity in a competitive landscape. Ultimately, the pursuit of excellence is a catalyst for personal fulfillment, organizational success, and the continuous elevation of standards and aspirations. That's powerful stuff.

And then, of course, there's **respect**, which goes hand-in-hand with humility. Respect is crucial for maintaining a harmonious and productive workplace. It means treating every individual with dignity and valuing their contributions, regardless of their position or background. Recognizing and honoring someone's essential worth as a human being. Dignity is inherent, not earned; it's a non-negotiable. We need to respect everyone's dignity, especially in these times, when it seems as if degrading others is part of the game.

I'm not talking about overlooking incompetence or ignoring the fact that someone isn't the right fit for your role or organization. This is about acknowledging and respecting everyone's worth as a human being, regardless of any factor of their identity—race, gender, sexual orientation, socioeconomic status, nationality, religion, age, ability, language, geography, education, occupation, family structure, cultural background, personal interests, political beliefs, and more. Only when we create a safe environment that honors everyone's dignity can people be their best selves and do their best work—for themselves and for the organization at large.

For me, respect is not just about how we treat others, but also how we treat ourselves. We've talked about the internal work we all must do as we confront our existing belief systems, including our cultural conditioning. When people choose not to do this work, they don't always have the capacity to respect themselves. On the flip side, the more you engage in behaviors consistent with your beliefs and values, the more confident you'll feel as a leader.

How does this translate to a work environment? Great leaders know that everyone has the potential to be a leader in their own right, and that every voice matters. They truly know that leadership is independent of position. As such, they work to create safe spaces where people can be accepted and acknowledged for who they are. They feel that they'll be valued and respected for what they bring to the table. As Marquette University Professor of Management Kristie Rogers writes in *Harvard Business Review*, "Employees who say they feel respected are more satisfied with their jobs and more grateful for—and loyal to—their companies. They are more resilient, cooperate more with others, perform better and more creatively, and are more likely to take direction from their leaders."[4]

This value is deeply connected to my spiritual belief in non-violence toward others and ourselves. I firmly believe that when we truly respect ourselves and the people around us, we create a culture of compassion and empathy. That's the kind of environment where everyone can thrive.

Respect is also a key ingredient in psychological safety, which Harvard Business School Professor of Leadership Amy Edmondson defines as "feeling safe to take interpersonal risks, to disagree openly, to surface concerns without fear of negative repercussions or pressure to sugarcoat bad news."[5] The benefits of psychological safety are tremendous. Psychological safety helps people feel good at work and with their peers, bolstering community and stoking innovation. But it doesn't just improve "the soft stuff: it substantially contributes to team effectiveness, learning, employee retention, and—most critically—better decisions and better performance."[6] In short, it supports the kind of environment many of us never thought possible. But it only works if everyone does the work. The same is true for core values.

For me, the core values of humility, collaboration, excellence, and respect are not just a motto on my website. I've actively lived them and worked to embed them into the DNA of every organization I've been a part of. These values guide how we make decisions, how we interact with one another, how we navigate challenges and triumphs as a team, and how we create successful businesses.

Sowing Seeds and Pulling Weeds

"Okay, Sheila," you say. "Humility, collaboration, excellence, and respect are great core values. But how do you know whether people are aligned with your values before you're actively working together? And how can you weed out the ones who aren't?"

It's a great question. A lot of it is about simply paying attention. Developing a high-performing culture is like cultivating a garden that needs constant tending. When assessing potential team members or an organization's culture, I pay close attention to actions and behaviors, especially during interviews. Since so many interactions today are virtual, that can make it more challenging, but even group video calls can provide a lot of useful information. I focus on how people treat others, the level of respect they show, and whether or not they create a sense of belonging for everyone in the room. Are they always interrupting and cutting people off or do they make room for others? Do they get defensive when others share feedback, or do they pause to take it in and respond thoughtfully? And do they just talk the talk, or do they walk the talk?!

If I'm with a candidate in person, I read body language, a move backed by science. Renowned body language researcher Albert Mehrabian found that a whopping 55 percent of communication is non-verbal, an assertion that's supported by numerous studies.[7] Do they appear closed off? Are their arms crossed over their chest during the interview? Do they pivot their body away, or do they lean in? If we go to a restaurant, I observe how they treat the servers. Are they domineering and demanding? Or are they kind and inclusive?

Further, do they mirror others' moves? When we see people take on a posture or expression, mirror neurons in our brains activate, making it feel as if we've taken a similar action. It's why others' moods can feel contagious; their behavior has a direct impact on the way we feel. Mirroring someone else's behavior creates a sense of commonality and thus puts us at ease. It can demonstrate that someone is tuned into you and indicate that they're willing to collaborate.[8]

If I complete my evaluation—taking all those factors into account—and don't like what I find, I don't move forward with that hire.

Sometimes, it's difficult to truly assess someone's fit during the interviewing process. We have all misjudged someone's capabilities or values or otherwise selected someone who was the wrong fit for whatever reason. That's part of the game. What's most important is that those of us in leadership roles ascertain these mismatches and make decisions early for the sake of the organization. We do our part to tend and cultivate our gardens even in these difficult circumstances, treating people who we ultimately must let go with the same respect we afford everyone in our organization. As Maya Angelou beautifully explained, "I've learned that people will forget what you said, people will forget what you did, but people will never forget how you made them feel."

By the same token, if you're in the hot seat, interviewing for a role yourself, pay attention to the people you meet—especially those in leadership positions. Are they diverse, representing different backgrounds, experiences, and perspectives? Are they kind, engaged, and open? Do they seem closed off or catty? Do you get whiffs of that toxicity we've talked about, or do you see yourself being able to flourish in their presence? Most importantly, can you imagine yourself running things one day, if that's your goal? This is especially important for people of diverse backgrounds.

> **Not all companies are made of glass walls and ceilings (or concrete ones, for that matter). Some are filled with mirrors, where you can see yourself, your talent, and drive reflected everywhere you look.**

Many leadership experts suggest considering whether you'll need to hide your true self to fit in—or even feel safe—at work. Ask yourself direct questions like: "Does my authenticity fit the culture?" "Do senior leaders insist on inclusive and diverse styles from the top down and the bottom up?" "Are men getting similar feedback as me, or is there noticeable gender bias?" These probing questions can provide valuable insight into whether the culture of a company can sustain your long-term career goals and professional development.

If you don't see a path to where you want to go with people who will help you get there, don't be afraid to go elsewhere! Find a company with amazing leaders who are ready and willing to invest in you. Remember that employees at all levels can make an impact on culture. You can vote with your feet, demanding what you want by refusing to settle for anything less.

And as you'll soon see, **not all companies are made of glass walls and ceilings (or concrete ones, for that matter). Some are filled with mirrors, where you can see yourself, your talent, and your drive reflected everywhere you look.** Life is too short to be somewhere where you—and others—can't see your potential.

Define Your Values

Your core values might be different from mine. That's great! The only thing that matters is that you identify and uphold values that are authentically yours. Whether you're building a team or joining one, you want to make sure your values align with the environment around you.

Rather than simply choosing values from a predefined list, I'd like to guide you through an exercise that helped me discover my own deeply held values—ones I might never have identified otherwise.

Here's what I'd like you to try: Take out a piece of paper or open your *Mirror Effect Workbook & Journal.* Instead of listing abstract concepts that sound good, we're going to uncover the values that are already guiding your life's high points.

Step 1: Think about three to five peak moments in your life. Times when you felt most alive, fulfilled, and truly yourself. These could be professional triumphs, personal milestones, or quiet moments of deep satisfaction. Jot down a brief description of each experience.

Step 2: For each high moment, ask yourself:

- What was happening in this moment?
- Why did this experience feel so meaningful to me?
- What need or desire was being fulfilled?
- What value was being honored in this situation?

Step 3: Look for patterns across your high-point experiences. What common themes emerge? What values appear repeatedly? These are your authentic core values—the principles that, when honored, make you feel most alive and aligned.

Our values serve as our power center, a strong grounding force that anchors us even in difficult times. When we compromise our values, we lose self-trust and our entire system becomes wobbly. This is why identifying your true values is so crucial. They're fundamental to maintaining your center when facing pressure to compromise.

I've found these values to be most powerful when I narrow them down to three to five core principles. Once you've identified yours, keep them close in whatever way works for you:

- Write them on a sticky note and place it on your bathroom mirror
- Jot them down on a card and slip it inside your bag or wallet
- Display them prominently on your desk at work

Having your values visible reminds you to check in: When something feels off in an interaction or situation, you can refer back to your core values and identify what's misaligned. This awareness is your first step toward creating a life and work environment that truly honors who you are.

Finding—and creating—a supportive environment must include a thorough evaluation of your values, no matter which ones you choose. In the cultures I've helped shape, our leadership has fostered humility, collaboration, excellence, and respect—and I've seen people accomplish extraordinary things. When these values become the bedrock of a supportive work environment, it empowers teams to flourish, builds a strong sense of community, and drives the organization toward sustainable long-term success.

Though it may sound pie-in-the-sky, there are plenty of real-life examples of companies that are committed to doing right by their employees—to creating an environment where everyone can thrive.

A Commitment to Cultural Excellence

Take Patagonia, a retail clothing company known for living its values. Founder Yvon Chouinard established Patagonia in 1973 with a commitment to creating an organization that put the planet—and his employees—first. The company has always considered the environment alongside its bottom line, investing in programs that champion environmental and animal welfare; enacting responsibility programs that "ensure that [its] products are produced under safe; fair, legal, and humane working conditions;" and being fully transparent about its facilities and suppliers, giving the public insight into how its clothes are produced.[9]

To prioritize people, the company's HR team begins its hiring process by reading resumes from the bottom up: looking at candidates' interests, hobbies, and volunteer work to see where their hearts and minds are at. They're also dedicated to fostering a culture where people can pursue their passions and bring their whole selves to work. The company's employee handbook is titled, "Let My People Go Surfing," and team members are encouraged to do just that. As VP of HR, finances, and legal, Dean Carter explains, "We hire people who love being outside … so when the surf's up, they're going to be surfing anyway. If we didn't have a Let My People Go Surfing policy, we'd have a lot of performance action plans." As Dean says, "We let them be the humans we hired."[10]

A direct effect of that flexible policy? Excellent retention, with a turnover rate of just 4 percent. It's the kind of place people want to stick around. And the ones who do, do their best work for the company.

Those decisions have also had a significant impact on Patagonia's bottom line, earning it a valuation of about $3 billion as of 2022. While others may have chosen to sell or go public, Chouinard continued to walk his talk, transferring his ownership of the company to a trust and non-profit organization that would continue to put the profits to good use, investing about $100 million per year in fighting climate change and preserving undeveloped land.[11]

With five consecutive years on the "World's Best Workplaces" list, Hilton Hotels and Resorts has long been serious about employees' quality of life, offering benefits like parental leave, adoption assistance, mental health and wellness support, and debt-free education programs.[12] But its efforts have also helped the company rank among the world's most equitable and woman-friendly companies. That's based on nearly 1.2 million employee survey responses, more than half of which were from women.[13] The company's efforts to cultivate an equitable workplace start at the top, with its commitment to "global gender parity and 25 percent ethnic diversity in corporate leadership by 2027."[14]

As of this writing, 50 percent of Hilton's board of directors are women, and its most senior leaders are involved in its diversity and inclusion efforts, helping to ensure that representation at every level is seen as an organizational priority. For example, the company launched its Executive Committee Networking Program to invest in the success of people with diverse backgrounds.[15] As part of the program, the company's executives, including president and CEO Chris Nassetta, meet with and mentor diverse emerging leaders.

Cisco is another frequent flier on lists of great places to work, hitting *Fortune*'s Best Companies to Work For® list for three years in a row for a whole host of reasons, including its focus on employee engagement. At Cisco, team members are encouraged to recognize each other, publicly acknowledging their peers for their great work—the effects of which include boosting collaboration, productivity, and employee satisfaction.[16] As one employee shared, "Cisco is truly a unique and special place where we feel both supported and encouraged to make suggestions, inspire change, and ultimately to be our authentic selves. Cisco powers my purpose to follow my passion and lead with impact."[17]

That's the kind of environment we all can aspire to, regardless of whether we're in a leadership role already or just starting our ascent of the corporate ladder. We all deserve the life of our dreams, and we owe it to ourselves—and to others—not to settle for anything else. It may still sound wild, but work can be a source of joy, contributing to our lives rather than holding us back. Remember, you're powerful beyond measure, and that means you have the potential to find and create that reality for yourself and for others.

Now you know that a great environment is a reality, let's imagine what that world could be for you—and talk about how to get there.

Are You Where You Want to Be?

Imagine a work environment where fear isn't the motivator, and safety and support are cornerstones of success. An environment where collaboration reigns supreme. An environment where your values align with the organization's, empowering you to flourish and prosper.

In a truly supportive setting, every voice counts. It's not just about speaking up—it's about shouting from the rooftops and having folks cheer you on. Instead of battling one another, you come together to achieve your goals. And it really feels as good as it sounds.

So how do you know if your current environment makes the grade? Ask yourself these questions:

- Do you wake up excited to go to work? Or do you wake up full of anxiety and dread?
- Does working with others in your organization leave you feeling energized and excited? Or deflated and defeated?
- Do you enjoy the work you're doing and feel valuable to those around you? Or do you feel like you're trapped in a vortex of negativity where you are devalued and diminished?
- Can you raise your voice and be heard? Or do you have to bite your tongue for fear of retribution?
- Is the focus on winning as a team? Or is it more like a WWE Smackdown between coworkers?

And if the answer to the second half of one or more of those questions is yes . . . is that truly where you want to be?

Work Your Magic

When we end up working where we truly want to be, we'll find out that being part of a supportive tribe feels magical. People genuinely celebrate each other's successes because we're all playing for the same team. We never set one another up for failure, only success. And it's not a one-way street; we all give and receive, creating a beautiful cycle of support and positivity. That allows each of us to tap into our true potential, and to rejoice when we see other team members spread their wings and soar.

The first time I was ever part of a real tribe was during my medical residency. Our program director espoused a culture of care and kindness toward each other and toward our patients. He truly modeled the Ubuntu philosophy of "I am because we are." Residency programs are known for cultivating a cutthroat culture, where overworked residents are constantly fighting for a spot at the top, but in mine, senior residents stepped up to help junior residents and interns make it through. At the end of a long shift, they would help us do our rounds and write notes so we could get home quicker, enabling us to get some much-needed sleep and come back to work refreshed.

Each new class of students paid this kindness forward, caring for the next one. We all did our part to advance that culture, further evidence that you can make an impact at any level.

Of course, you can't always heal a toxic environment. Even the most gifted captain can't always save a sinking ship. But you do have the opportunity to lead, regardless of your title. Think about what you can do to create an environment where individuals feel safe, respected, and valued—and then *enlist others in your mission*. If you have a role in hiring and firing, always keep your values top of mind. And when difficult situations arise, as they will, choose empathy and compassion. Addressing challenges and conflicts from a calm, centered place fosters an environment where people can ask questions and speak up if something doesn't feel right. That's how you grow and evolve and equip others to do the same.

I learned this for myself over the course of many years. As I gained more experience in my career, I realized the importance of slowing down and being more mindful in my interactions. In the past, I might have glossed over certain behaviors, dismissing them as normal or expected. But now I take a moment to ground myself and ask how I truly feel about a situation. I've become more attuned to my own boundaries and what I want from my work environment. It was liberating to finally recognize that I get to choose my environment. To ask myself, "Who do I want to work with, and what kind of workplace do I envision?" If I see any red flags—like feeling threatened or pressured to conform to someone else's expectations—I don't hesitate to act.

Ultimately, being more mindful and deliberate in my choices has allowed me to cultivate a deeper understanding of the people I work with and the environments I engage in. I'm no longer willing to overlook behaviors that don't align with my values, and I'm not afraid to seek out opportunities that truly nurture my growth and well-being. It's a continuous journey of self-discovery, but it has led me to find greater fulfillment and satisfaction in both my personal and professional life.

Perfect Is Overrated. Imperfection Is Growth.

Before I wrap up this chapter, let me make one thing clear: There's no such thing as a perfect work environment. So don't focus on creating a utopia; use your energy to build a community on a foundation of support and authenticity. No one's infallible, and no culture can claim to be flawless. Life will always throw disruptions, uncertainties, and unforeseen curveballs our way. And sometimes, despite our best intentions to create and/or work in a thriving culture, we may fall short or fail outright.

That's okay. Sometimes the true test of an organization is not how they respond in good times, but how they weather the storms. Do they revert to old habits and patterns of behavior when the wind starts blowing? Or do they all row together, coming out stronger on the other side?

The expectation of perfection is itself toxic. It's like chasing a mirage in the desert: It'll leave you parched and frustrated. Instead, we must learn to embrace the imperfections and the messiness of life. Failure is not the end; it's just another stepping stone on the road to success. And in a truly supportive environment, failure is not feared but rather met with optimism. Only by stumbling can we learn to fly.

Step into Your Power

To find the right environment—one where you can thrive, constantly leveling up to achieve what you once thought to be impossible—you've got to know what "right" feels like to you. That can be hard after a lifetime of conforming to others' expectations, but it *is* possible. To begin:

- **Start with a vision.** The first step in finding an environment you love is knowing what you want it to look like and what you hope to achieve.
- **Identify your values and stick to them.** If you can find an environment that aligns with those values, you're in a good spot. If you're in the position to build the environment yourself, keep those values front-of-mind in every decision you make.
- **Ask yourself honest questions.** What's your energy level when you come to work? Do you wake up with excitement or dread? No job is perfect, and some days are better than others, so your energy won't be a ten out of ten all the time. But if you see consistent patterns emerging in the way you feel about your job, don't push them aside.

- **You deserve an environment where you can step into your full power.** Do what you need to do to take care of yourself, which might mean carefully considering your options before you head out the door. Just remember that, in the long run, you deserve to work in a healthy, supportive environment. Don't settle for anything less. You deserve everything you've ever dreamed of, and you have the power to make it happen.
- **Co-creation is the name of the game.** You can be the catalyst for a supportive work environment, but you can't turn the tide alone. Find allies who will partner with you to build something great. And if you can't find any, that's valuable information, too.

In Part I, we learned how to do the internal work of knowing ourselves. We faced our FIDS and emerged with more compassion toward ourselves.

In Part II, we turned that awareness and compassion outward, learning to navigate complicated work environments and opening our eyes to what's really going on. We honed and sharpened our skills of perception, clarity, and insight.

In Part III, we'll put the two together. I'll share secrets for creating a "personal board of directors" that see and value your authentic self. We'll delve into how to negotiate successfully so that you're creating wins for everyone. And we'll talk about managing your energy at work so you can be the best version of yourself and feel truly, totally happy.

Rubber, meet road. Time to put your badass skills into practice and set yourself up for success.

PART III

MAKE A LIFE WORTH MIRRORING:
SET YOURSELF UP FOR SUCCESS

CHAPTER 9

SURROUND YOURSELF WITH MIRRORS

Building Your Personal Board of Directors

> **"I feel really grateful to the people who encouraged me and helped me develop. Nobody can succeed on their own."**
>
> *–Sheryl Sandberg*

'll cut right to the chase: Even when you know who you are and that you're powerful beyond measure, you can't do it all by yourself. It's a lesson I've learned over and over again from the brilliant, talented, passionate mentors, mentees, sponsors, role models, and subject-matter experts I've known over the years. All of us—even the very best in our businesses—need people we can turn to in all seasons: when the going gets tough and when the getting is good.

These people serve as our mirrors, reflecting back our true capabilities, potential, and strengths, including ones we sometimes cannot see ourselves. They show us who we really are and who we can become. When we doubt ourselves or can't recognize our own brilliance, these mirrors hold up a clear reflection of our value and power. Without them in our lives, we risk living with a distorted view of ourselves—either underestimating our abilities or failing to see areas where growth is needed.

Hillary Clinton's book *It Takes a Village* may have focused primarily on the resources needed to effectively raise children, but it also highlighted the fact that we must depend on each other to grow successfully and effectively.

A talented young woman I know, Cheyenne, learned that lesson firsthand just a few years ago. Cheyenne was a rising star who'd worked her way up from an entry-level role to a junior leadership position at a financial firm in just one year. Her supervisor recognized her potential after seeing her talent for identifying challenges and creating innovative solutions. Now Cheyenne was responsible for analyzing larger issues and presenting findings to senior leaders at regular meetings.

It was a great opportunity, but imposter syndrome held her back. Talking to her small team had been easy; they were all at similar levels. But presenting to senior leaders felt intimidating. Many had decades of experience in finance and established personal lives. Cheyenne, just a few years out of school, felt like she didn't belong in those rooms. She wondered how she could confidently engage with them one-on-one, let alone present to a packed boardroom.

Cheyenne decided to start small by finding one approachable leader. She listened for personal details in pre-meeting small talk and looked for conversation openers—someone leaving with a tennis racket, a desk photo, anything revealing their interests.

She set her sights on Diane, who always carried leadership books. One afternoon, seeing Diane with Simon Sinek's *Start with Why*, Cheyenne stopped her.

"Hi, Diane. I've been meaning to read that! Would you recommend it?"

This simple question sparked a conversation. Diane was delighted to discuss books and leadership development with a junior staff member. She suggested Cheyenne read the book herself and invited her to chat about it afterward. Two weeks later, Cheyenne arrived prepared, articulating her thoughts on the book's application to their firm, and mentioned another title Diane might enjoy.

Eventually, Cheyenne asked Diane to be her mentor. Diane was honored, and they began meeting regularly to discuss leadership, speaking skills, and problem-solving. Because she felt comfortable with Diane—a senior executive who validated her ideas—Cheyenne grew more confident around other leaders, too. Diane had become an essential mirror for Cheyenne, reflecting back a version of herself she couldn't yet see clearly—a capable professional whose ideas and presence belonged in those senior leadership meetings. Each time Diane validated Cheyenne's thinking or praised her work, that reflection grew clearer, helping Cheyenne's self-image align with her true capabilities.

What Cheyenne didn't realize was that Diane advocated for her even in rooms Cheyenne couldn't access, which led to more professional opportunities.

With newfound confidence, Cheyenne developed another valuable connection with Bill, an expert in market trend analysis. Though they had little in common personally, she knew his expertise could help her thrive. He was flattered by her interest and happy to help with challenges she faced in her work.

Seeing the impact of finding people willing to invest in her success, Cheyenne was inspired to pay it forward. She formed a group for early and mid-level employees interested in skill development. This yielded even more connections with people ready to support her—professionals of all ages with different skill sets who helped her advance in various ways. When she encountered people doing what she aspired to do, she thoughtfully considered how they could enhance her experience and how she could support them, then reached out.

That's how you build a personal board. And it's one of the best resources you can have.

The Personal Board as Disco Ball

Think of a personal board as a group you bring together to help run the businesses of your career—and your life. **When you've assembled diverse,** talented individuals ready to help make your dreams happen, you unlock countless resources and opportunities. Together, these individuals form a sophisticated mirror system, each reflecting different aspects of your potential and capabilities—like a disco ball. Unlike a single flat mirror that shows just one perspective, this multi-faceted reflection gives you a complete, three-dimensional view of yourself. Some mirrors reflect your technical skills, others your leadership abilities, and still others your interpersonal strengths. Collectively, they help you see yourself whole and complete, often more accurately than you can see yourself. These people have the knowledge to help you grow, the connections to open doors, the kindness to have your back, and the willingness to advocate for you.

> When you've assembled diverse, talented individuals ready to help make your dreams happen, you unlock countless resources and opportunities.

You can learn from their paths to success, including how to avoid their pitfalls. You can leverage their expertise, expand your industry knowledge, and get valuable advice about moves—big and small—that will make a difference in your career. Board members serve as excellent sounding boards for both problems and solutions, helping you set goals and hold yourself accountable while celebrating your milestones. They can coach your communication skills and boost your confidence, as Diane did for Cheyenne, while expanding your network and increasing your reach. And with all those mirrors in place, you'll find yourself operating in technicolor.

You can see how a thoughtfully compiled board has the potential to accelerate your journey to success. But building one can be tricky, particularly for women and people from other historically marginalized groups. With a dearth of us in high-ranking leadership positions—just 25 percent of CEOs are women, and only 17 percent of the C-Suite are BIPOC—it can be hard to find board members who get where you're coming from.[1] We also face discrimination at every turn.

For example, a study published in *Harvard Business Review* showed that women face age bias, regardless of how old they are.[2] The study found that young women—those under forty—faced a "credibility deficit" and weren't taken seriously by their colleagues. (If you've ever been called "kiddo" by a guy with gray hair, you know what I mean.)[3] Meanwhile, those considered "middle aged"—between the ages of forty and sixty—were told they had too many family responsibilities, and even discriminated against due to "menopause-related issues."[4] And those older than sixty described feeling "discounted" and "irrelevant" due to their age. So it makes sense that, according to *Forbes*, "There is a pronounced gender discrepancy when it comes to American mentorship; 82 percent of men have had male mentors, while just 69 percent of women have had female mentors."[5]

That said, it can be incredibly meaningful to have a trusted team who knows where you're coming from, who understands what it's like to work your way up the ranks without the benefits of an automatic Boys' Club membership or a working knowledge of pickleball. We each have unique needs, insights, ideas, and trajectories, and having support from people who understand that is priceless. That's why, when it comes to building your board, you have to know where to look—and how to connect. It's often not as easy as waltzing into the office kitchen with some weekend sports stats tucked into your back pocket (although it may not hurt to do that, either).

With that in mind, let's talk about how to build a board that will really work for you.

Build Your Board

If you haven't yet, you've got to take some time to think about what you really want from your life and career. After all, you need to know where you're going before you figure out who can help get you there.

- What roles would you like to have throughout your career?

- What areas of expertise do you want to keep developing?
- What do you want to learn more about?
- How do you want your work life to integrate with your personal life?

Let me elaborate a little on that last question. For example, do you see yourself having kids and taking time off to raise them? Do you envision yourself taking a short leave and coming right back, ready to rock and roll? Would you rather prioritize personal fulfillment and travel over parenting, exploring the world for a handful of months—or even years—at a time? The options are endless, but you've got to know which are most appealing to you.

Once you have your answers, it's time to scope out potential board contenders and see what they have to offer.

Your personal board of directors should ideally have these five types of members:

- **Supporters.** Supporters are people who have your back no matter what. Think of them as your own personal cheerleading squad, the people willing to celebrate your accomplishments and build you up on your lowest days. You're not afraid to let them see you cry, and those tears don't scare them either. They're there to build you up when you need it, reminding you of your power and what you're poised to accomplish.
- **Sponsors.** Sponsors are willing to go to bat for you, singing your praises in those rooms you don't yet have access to. They mention your name when you're not present and throw your hat in the ring for exclusive opportunities, championing your biggest successes to others.

- **Mentors.** Mentors are there to help you progress, giving you the advice and resources you need to level up. They tell it like it is. They've run the gauntlet in your chosen industry, and they can help you play the game by offering valuable advice, insights, and feedback on your performance and behavior.

- **Role models.** You don't have to know—or have deep personal relationships with—everyone who will have an impact on your career. Role models serve as an example of who you want to be or what you'd like to achieve. You can learn from their work by studying their careers or seeking out the thought leadership they, or those they admire, put out into the world. Books, podcasts, lectures, interviews, and case studies can provide vital insight into what they did to get where they are, and help you chart a similar course.

- **Subject-matter experts:** Subject-matter experts have deep knowledge in a particular area or set of areas and thus can add a lot of value on your personal board. Think accountants, financial advisors, lawyers, or experts in your field (like Cheyenne's colleague Bill)—people who can give you insight that stems from their area of study and expertise.

Some people on your board may wear multiple hats, but everyone needs at least one of them. Just as you'd want with an organization's board, yours should be diverse, representing a variety of experiences, expertise, and backgrounds. Keep in mind that boards of all sorts tend to change over time. Members shift, as do their roles. Sometimes, people will surprise you. Those you thought were your sponsors will turn out to be mentors instead—willing to give you advice but not advocate for you. And, on the flip side, some sponsors will seemingly emerge out of the ether. Time and again, people I assumed weren't even thinking about me were quick to share my name in the rooms I wasn't in. When I came to understand that different people could play different roles on my board—and that sometimes those roles would shift—a lightbulb went off. I leaned into the dynamism of it all, and made sure that when I asked for help, I was asking the right people for the right things. And when those relationships did change, I respected those adjustments, while making an effort to keep in contact with those who played less prominent roles than they had before.

> *The Mirror Effect Workbook & Journal* helps you map your current support network and identify gaps in your personal board of directors. Through targeted exercises, you'll assess which roles need filling and develop strategies for building meaningful connections with potential supporters, sponsors, and mentors.

Conduct Your Search

So, with all that in mind, how do you know who fits the bill when it comes to each role?

Look to people inside and outside your current company, and think about what role they might play based on what they do, what insights they may have to offer, and if they could be supporters, sponsors, mentors, role models, or subject-matter experts. While supporters can come from any facet of your life, having a sponsor at work can be particularly helpful—especially if they have pull at your company. They can open doors by mentioning your name when a new opportunity arises, call out your achievements in meetings, and help you navigate workplace politics. But having sponsors outside the office can be beneficial, too. Individuals from other organizations can expand your horizons, introducing you to new opportunities, ways of thinking, and connections beyond the four walls of your organization. If you've been feeling like you're not in the right place, a sponsor stationed elsewhere can help you make your next career move.

Like supporters, mentors can come from anywhere; if they have the experience and expertise to advise you in an area where you want to grow, you're on the right track. The same goes for role models, particularly because you don't need to know them in real life to benefit from their insights.

Don't hesitate to crowdsource subject-matter experts from your existing community. A colleague or friend may have a great recommendation for an expert who supports them now or has in the past. A little online research also goes a long way in this department.

You can start to build your board by making a list of people who could be good supporters, sponsors, mentors, role models, and subject-matter experts. People like:

- Senior executives at your company
- Those who have held your current role in the past
- People in roles you aspire to hold
- People who you admire
- Experts in an area where you currently excel
- Experts in areas you want to learn more about

Jot down people in your immediate network and ones in networks you want to be a part of. Research others using LinkedIn. Don't be afraid to think big—that's the only way to make big things happen.

Next, get more specific:

- Who are you connected to currently?
- Who are your connections' connections? (Regularly update this as you expand your network.)
- Who are those dream connections?

Think about how you can connect with people outside of your immediate and extended networks. What conferences or networking events can you attend? What organizations, groups, or clubs can you join at your alma mater, at work, or in your industry? Is there anyone out there who may be worth cold calling? Someone who may be inspired by your story and eager to lend a hand? These efforts will help you extend your network quickly and reach people you don't have direct or indirect access to at the moment.

Last list, I promise. To find great role models, you can do a little research and keep your criteria broad when it comes to accessibility. Maybe you're moved by Jenna Lyons's steady climb through the ranks of J. Crew and the way she's transformed her career—and style at large—in the years since she left. Perhaps you're inspired by Michelle Obama's wise approach to improving health and well-being through movement. Or perhaps you admire Girls Who Code founder Reshma Saujani's commitment to reforming the corporate world to create a more equitable environment for women. You have access to so much of their brilliance if you're willing to do just a bit of digging. Find the stuff they've put out into the world and make a plan to dive in.

Then, it's time to take action.

Overcome Self-Doubt

Reaching out to potential mentors and sponsors can feel overwhelming. I remember my palms sweating when I was a young medical resident, eager to talk to an attending physician I admired. She had an incredible bedside manner and constantly thought outside the box. I felt as if she was light years ahead of me in every way.

If you're walking in similar shoes, you may be thinking about all the reasons a potential board member may not want to hear from you. Maybe you worry it would be an imposition, or that you're not worthy of their time. Maybe you don't want to rock the boat with your current supervisor by reaching out to someone multiple levels ahead of you. Maybe it feels like too big of an ask, especially of someone so busy and important. But the thing is, you *are* worthy. You're powerful beyond measure, and that means you have incredible potential and remarkable insights to add to the conversation, even if you're new to it.

Plus, your potential board members have been where you are. They know what it's like. And they want to share what they know; they get something out of the exchange, too. I often feel that *I'm* the one who gets the most out of mentoring sessions, even though I'm there to help someone else. It's an honor to help someone shift their perspective for the better, or to give them the strength to manage a difficult situation or uncover their greatness and ultimately find success. And so many of us have benefited from mentors of our own and *want* to pay it forward—just as you will someday. (If not already.) So many of us want to build a world that's better for all of us, to shift the paradigm so that eventually, no one will need a book like this one. That's certainly my goal.

But early in my career, before I knew all that, I worked up the courage to chat with the attending physician I mentioned. After that, she took a special interest in me and became the first member of my personal board. Her honest advice is one reason I made a big move in my medical career. If I hadn't gotten past my initial fear of approaching her, I might not have had the insight or courage I needed to make that bold move.

Over the years, my board grew. A senior partner at McKinsey and mother of four helped me think about how to navigate parenting and career, letting me learn from the choices she made and helping me consider the challenges and opportunities out there. Today, my oldest child is approaching college, and we're still in touch.

Others helped me chart a path in biotech, serving as supporters, sponsors, and mentors in spaces I hadn't yet been. And numerous executive coaches, who served as supporters, mentors, and subject-matter experts, helped me grow and learn from my successes, missed opportunities, and mistakes—and some of theirs—along the way. One company coach helped me realize I wasn't in the right environment and encouraged me to find a role that checked all my boxes, even though it meant that I'd leave the organization. She cared enough to help me find a place where I could truly thrive.

These board members took an interest in me for all kinds of reasons—a shared identity, a spiritual connection, a similar focus—but each connection was born out of me overcoming self-doubt and leaning into opportunity. That brings us to networking.

The Power of Networking

I was on a panel for 50/50 Women on Boards—a nonprofit organization that aims to improve diversity on corporate boards—when I was asked how I secured my first board position. I shared the three pieces of advice that helped me do it:

1. Be excellent at what you do—something you're known for in your industry.
2. Be strategic. What kind of seat do you want? Why do you want it? What do you think you could do if you got it? And importantly, who can help you secure it?
3. Network, network, network. Put your intentions out there, telling anyone who might be able to help exactly what you're interested in.

This third piece of the puzzle, networking, is crucial. We can't talk about building a personal board without broaching the subject of networking, something that's proven tremendously important when it comes to women's success in particular.

Business intelligence company Morning Consult conducted a survey of 751 women leaders to determine the impact of networking on their careers and business outcomes.[6] It found that "networking not only plays pivotal roles in achieving nearly every career milestone from achieving a board seat to breaking into the C-Suite, but also drives broader operational and revenue benefits for their organizations."[7]

A whopping 80 percent of the women surveyed reported that the connections they made during networking events or through networking groups helped them secure transformative roles. Networking gave them a path to everything from C-suite jobs to board positions and provided valuable support to improve their quality of life at work and beyond. It helped them secure raises at their current jobs and even identify and land roles with better work-life balance.[8] And while we assume that networking can happen anywhere, Morning Consult's research found that it was in formal networking environments—events, professional networking groups, conferences, trade associations, and so on—that these pivotal relationships are formed. Further, those with intersectional identities reaped even more benefits from networking than their peers.

But it's not just individual women who benefit from these networking efforts. Research shows that "the advancement of women into senior leadership drives firm performance, profitability, and diversity."[9] Altrata's 2022 Global Gender Diversity report also showed that having a woman CEO or board chair had a significant impact on gender parity throughout their organizations.[10] Women pay forward the benefits they glean from networking, with their organizations being major beneficiaries: "More than 70 percent have used networking to achieve organizational goals such as winning new business (85 percent), implementing new frameworks or models (84 percent), leading successful projects (82 percent), improving processes (76 percent), and saving money for their team or organization (74 percent)."[11]

Who were the best networkers of the bunch? Those at the executive level. Survey results showed that executives were more likely than middle management leaders to reap the benefits of their networking efforts due to superior skills in that area, including "choosing purpose-driven opportunities and engaging with their core networking group at least weekly, if not daily."[12]

How do you improve your networking skills, particularly if you haven't reached the upper echelon of your organization or industry?

Small Talk Leads to Big Talk

Tapping into those formal groups is key, but don't hesitate to reach out to people you meet elsewhere! Tell them you're interested in talking to them, ask if they'll have coffee or lunch, or drop by their office if it feels appropriate. Your future board members are likely really busy, so take what you can get. And then let things unfold.

I'm not saying it will be easy, but it *will* get easier. As Cheyenne's experience demonstrates, it only takes one person to change how an entire organization perceives you—and how you perceive yourself. Better yet, it often takes one small thing to get started: breaking the ice. I'm talking about small talk, chatting about the incidentals of our lives. While the idea of small talk may make you cringe, it can have a tremendous impact on what you can accomplish, and that makes it an art worth considering.

A parent recently described a conversation he had with his son. His son was talking about how much he hated small talk, that he'd rather do almost anything than chat about the weather or something equally minor—dental work included.

"Son," he said, "small talk leads to big talk." So often, we need small talk to develop the kind of trust and intimacy necessary to go deeper or make a significant ask. That's why most mentoring relationships start organically—61 percent of them to be exact.[13]

Of course, small talk can be tricky when you don't have a lot in common. When you're not a part of the majority in an environment, it's hard to find common interests. Maybe you don't follow the same sports (I personally know very little about golf, and I plan to keep it that way), or like the same music, or even have the same style when it comes to fashion. It can be difficult to find a way in when you don't feel like you fit in.

The key is finding common ground, and there's usually some of it, *somewhere*. Remember, though, that you're not looking to chat with just anyone. You want to find the *right* board members, people who will contribute to your work and life in real and meaningful ways. That means being more strategic, even with small talk. As you review your list of board candidates, ask yourself:

- What is one small thing we have in common, work-related or personal?
- What is a question I have about a topic in which they're an expert?
- What situation have they been in that I may encounter?
- Do I have a technical question for them about our shared company or industry?

Once you've initiated the conversation, ask follow-up questions to keep them engaged. But don't force it. If the conversation lulls, that's okay. You can always thank them for their time and excuse yourself. Maybe you come back at a later date. And if there's really nothing there, maybe you decide that individual isn't right for your board. If the interaction feels forced, they're probably not going to be a true supporter, sponsor, or mentor for you. I've certainly thought people were there for me, only to find out that they weren't for one reason or another. Try not to take it personally, just keep going. At the end of the day, it's all about trial and error.

Give Early and Often

With that said, knowing you have something to contribute helps. When you're making an ask, you should be thinking about how you can add to the exchange. How can you give back to someone you're hoping will offer so much to you? When you make the interaction valuable for them too, you lay the groundwork for a long-standing relationship and help allay any feelings that you're not pulling your weight.

Organizational psychologist Adam Grant has conducted extensive research on relationships, which he details in his book *Give and Take*. He found that there are three types of people: givers, takers, and matchers. Takers are always looking to get as much as possible out of an interaction, while giving back as little as they can, hoping that will help them achieve their goal as quickly as possible. On the other hand, givers "actually prefer to be on the contributing end of an interaction," offering up their resources without expectations. But, as Grant explains, most of us don't fall to either extreme; the majority of us are matchers: "A matcher is somebody who tries to maintain an even balance of give and take. If I help you, I expect you to help me in return."[14]

Who fares best when it comes to success?

It turned out those who did worst were most likely to be givers. Putting others first tends to land you at the bottom of the barrel. It's easy to find yourself tapped out or drained by takers, but takers didn't tend to end up at the top either, often burning their bridges in attempts to rise above others. Grant found that matchers would get caught up in their desires for a just world, looking to punish takers who take advantage of others and promote givers for their incredible generosity. And that actually *helped* givers. As a result, those at the top were most often givers! Givers turned out to be both the best and the worst!

What makes for a successful giver, versus an unsuccessful one? As Grant explains, when they meet someone new, they "try to figure out, 'How can I add value to this person's life, and what could I possibly contribute that might benefit this person?' What that typically means is they end up creating a lot of good will in the relationship...that often lies dormant until they may actually need it."[15]

If you can go into an interaction thinking about what you can give rather than what you can get, chances are you'll wind up better off. To avoid giving too much of yourself—and not getting enough back—Grant recommends the five-minute favor. Instead of giving everyone everything you've got, ask yourself if you can give them something uniquely valuable that will take you five minutes or less.[16]

Another way to be a successful giver? Be what Grant calls "otherish": concerned about helping others, while keeping your "own interests in the rearview mirror."[17] To do that, look for win-wins, opportunities to benefit others that are low cost to you, or that hold some mutual benefit. Taking an "otherish" approach makes your generosity sustainable rather than draining—and sets you up for success.

But how do you start the conversation? How do you get to the point where you have the opportunity to give (and, of course, to take)?

If at First You Don't Succeed, Try, Try Again

A big reason to cultivate esteemed and experienced personal board members is to learn from them. I wrote this book so you could learn from my mistakes. Others may sign on to be your mentor so you can learn from theirs. But even with all the information in the world, you're not going to be perfect—none of us are. We all slip up from time to time; it's getting back up and taking the steps to avoid the pain the next time around that gets us farther along.

In the case of building your board, trial and error may mean putting yourself out there and getting burned, asking someone to participate in your present and future and hearing "no." It could mean choosing people who aren't the best fit for your board. Perhaps their expertise isn't exactly right for what you're trying to accomplish. Maybe they don't have the time or the interest to invest in you in a real way. Ultimately, it's up to you to pull the plug.

Maybe they aren't doing what they said they would do. If your board members aren't walking the talk—if they're saying they're there for you but failing to come through, or if the relationship feels conditional—it may be time to walk away.

Or maybe the relationship has just run its course. That happens to all of us; it's part of the game. If you're not getting value anymore, you may need to wean the relationship over time, letting everyone off the hook.

Know when to call it (in a kind and respectful way of course) and take the time to understand where things went wrong so you can do better next time. Many times, the only way to get better is to go through it. And the quicker you do, the better off you'll be.

Learning through trial and error will also help you grow your board more quickly, evaluating who may or may not be right to join—or stay—so you can proceed accordingly.

As I mentioned, the goal should be to build a personal board that continues to grow, evolving into a network and eventually a community. You're building a safe place where you feel like you belong, surrounded by supporters, sponsors, and mentors who are dedicated to your well-being. That's where you can truly be your best.

As you take on more senior roles, the stakes only get higher, making your board even more important. So, find those board members and look for more, growing your community alongside your personal and professional aspirations. When you start to make headway, pay it forward, lifting others up as you climb and making them a part of your community, so everyone wins.

Step into Your Power

Building and managing your board is an ever-evolving process that will shift as your career and goals do. But understanding the value of the board itself—and who can play a key part in helping you level up—will prove invaluable as you navigate work and life.

- **Know your roles.** Think about who might be best for your board, convening a diverse group that reflects your interests, aspirations, and values. Focus on whether they'll contribute to your personal and professional growth as supporters, sponsors, mentors, role models, or subject-matter experts.

- **Embrace change.** The key players on your board will likely shift, sometimes occupying different roles than you anticipated or leaving their seats behind altogether. That's okay. Appreciate your board members for the role they've played and keep in touch. You never know when things may change, or someone may come through in a manner you didn't expect.

- **Challenge self-doubt.** Remind yourself of your worth and capabilities, even when you're approaching people who are more experienced than you. If you find your confidence flagging, remember that helping you benefits them, too.

- **Network, network, and network some more.** Research has shown that networking can be invaluable to your career, particularly if you're a woman. Putting yourself out there may be uncomfortable at first, but it offers myriad benefits with long-term effects. Get out of your comfort zone and give it a try. Like anything, the more you practice, the easier it will be.

- **Give and take—but mostly give.** Research shows that those at the bottom *and* top of the ladder are givers. Always think about how you can contribute to others, but don't compromise yourself in the process. That's how you create mutually beneficial relationships.

- **Expand your tribe.** Grow your network relentlessly as your career advances, and lift others up as you go.

Who you know matters quite a lot, but how you show up makes a difference, too. Of course, everything you do at work and beyond, including building and managing a personal board, takes negotiation. You've got to understand what you want, what you don't, and where you're willing to compromise. Let's talk about how to negotiate so you're ready for anything that comes your way.

CHAPTER 10

MASTER NEGOTIATIONS
Getting What You Want Without Compromising Yourself

"Power's not given to you. You have to take it."

–Beyoncé Knowles

t had been a typical Tuesday morning when Liat's desk phone rang. She'd woken up while it was still dark to get a workout and meditation session in, prepped the kids' lunches, left instructions for her husband on where to find the cleats for soccer practice that afternoon, and how to give the dog her medication so she'd actually take it. She'd gotten to work just before 7:30 a.m. so she could prepare for a full day's worth of meetings and presentations. And then, at 9:30 a.m., two hours into her office groove, HR was on the line.

"We're working on a significant salary adjustment for you," the rep told her. Liat was surprised—she hadn't asked for a raise.

Liat had been working for a high-profile marketing agency for a handful of years. When she'd been offered the role, she hadn't negotiated; she thought the pay was fair considering her experience. She knew, anecdotally, that she made a lot more money than most of the women she knew. And as one of the few female leaders at her firm, she didn't want to rock the boat.

Liat knew that she did excellent work, and her clients had confirmed this. Her reviews were stellar, so much so that she'd gotten a number of promotions with what she had thought to be reasonable pay bumps and bonuses over the years. If anything, she was outperforming her colleagues. So she wasn't quite sure why HR was calling her right then. "Can I ask about the reason for the adjustment?" she inquired.

It turned out that she was the lowest-paid employee in her group—by far. Her peers had been making much, much more than her; hundreds of thousands of dollars more, money that was compounding with each percentage-based raise they got. She was the outlier, and by so much that HR had flagged it.

The rep told her that they'd be adjusting her pay over the next few quarters, giving her incremental raises so she could enter the range where her peers had been since day one.

The news felt like a punch to the gut. She'd trusted that she'd been given a great offer, one that aligned with her worth. Her supervisors had never mentioned any discrepancy, not even once, even as they were praising her in front of the group and adjusting her title and responsibilities accordingly. She'd been too trusting, she realized, and now all she felt was hurt and betrayal.

But the conversation resulted in an important shift for her: Liat wouldn't take her compensation for granted anymore. She couldn't just let her talent and track record speak for themselves and leave her financial fate in the hands of her bosses. She knew she had to ask questions, understand salary benchmarks for her market, and advocate for herself from the very beginning if she wanted a fair shake, now or in the future.

With every subsequent opportunity, she paid close attention to the compensation the company was offering, considering not just the salary, but also bonuses, equity, and benefits. She did her research—learning the standard compensation benchmarks for similar companies and specific roles within those companies—so she could gauge how fair each offer was. As a high performer, she knew she should be pulling in more than the median rate, too. When she was offered anything less than what she knew she was worth, she spoke up.

When she reached the C-suite a few years later and took on her first board role, she paid careful attention to severance terms, change-of-control provisions, and other important terms that would be negotiated as part of her contract.

She didn't always get exactly what she asked for, of course. Negotiation is about give and take. But she refused to settle for an unfair rate. After all, as she'd learned, no one else would look out for her; she had to do it herself. It was her responsibility to ensure she was being treated the way she should be treated.

Liat realized that learning the ins and outs of negotiating had other benefits. It boosted her self-esteem and taught her to value herself. She was no longer looking for others to validate her worth. And when she got an answer she didn't like, she was not as reactive as she had once been. In the past, when things didn't go her way, she'd get emotional or angry or embarrassed, feeling foolish for putting herself out there. Now she realized it wasn't personal, and that she had the agency to respond or move on as she saw fit.

The fact is, you—like Liat—have options. Whether you're negotiating your pay at a new job, discussing the details of a salary adjustment as you accept a promotion, or collaborating with your board to take your business to the next level, you have the power to decide how you want to move forward.

Of course, there are times when taking a step back is appropriate. You may take a pay cut to break into a new industry or work with a different type of company, for instance. Or, you may have to concede to your company's board on certain points to move forward with an important initiative. But you don't have to settle for less than you're worth or compromise the fundamentals of who you are—or what your company is about—to fit neatly into someone else's box. When you step into your power and claim what's rightfully yours, in a way that feels authentic to you, the right people will respect you for it and you won't have to question yourself.

Additionally, having strong negotiation skills—something many women and members of numerous other disenfranchised groups don't get the chance to practice—is critical to your success as you level up. Essentially, anytime you're engaged in a strategic discussion with two or more parties to resolve an issue in a way that each party finds acceptable, you're negotiating. You must be able to negotiate for yourself, of course, but also on behalf of groups and organizations. This is key when it comes to founding companies, closing deals, and negotiating internally and externally.

I understand if this sounds like a pipe dream. So many of the people I've mentored over the years have felt the same way. But when you know what's behind your hesitance—and how to get past it—you're well on your way to negotiating a whole new reality for yourself.

Consider the rest of this chapter your playbook. Note that, while much of what we'll discuss references compensation specifically, the strategies and tactics we'll talk about apply to any type of negotiation. So without further ado, let's get into it.

Why Women Don't Negotiate

Negotiations are an essential component of doing business, but so few of us have been set up for success in that department. That's particularly true for women. In *Women Don't Ask: Negotiation and the Gender Divide*, authors Linda Babcock and Sara Laschever examine the social norms and constraints that have prevented women from getting what they want and need through effective negotiations. They found that women are 2.5 times more likely than men to say they feel "a great deal of apprehension" when it comes to negotiating. It's unsurprising, then, that men "initiate negotiations about four times as often as women."[1] That likely begins with how they conceptualize negotiating. While men described navigating negotiations as "winning a ball game" or a "wrestling match," women compared the process to "going to the dentist."[2]

Why do we feel this way?

In so many cases, we're conditioned to compromise, not make our case. Women also worry about feeling rejection if things don't go their way, and about how they'll be perceived (a very real concern, as you'll see in just a moment).[3] As such, we're less likely to negotiate, with 20 percent of women saying they never do it, even when it feels appropriate. For example, one study focused on graduating MBA students found that half of men negotiated their job offers, compared to just one-eighth of women.[4]

Women also go into negotiations with lower expectations about the amount of money or resources actually on the table. So we ask for less and ultimately get less—an average of 30 percent less than men.[5] Over time, that adds up. Those who don't negotiate their first salaries are likely to lose more than $500,000 by the time they hit sixty years old.[6]

On the flip side, those who do ask for more tend to get it. One study found that, of the women who did negotiate their salaries, 71 percent were successful.[7] In Lean In's Women in the Workplace 2019 study, which polled more than 64,000 women across 279 companies, researchers found that just specifying an amount could make a difference, as those who ask for a specific amount receive more than those who don't.[8]

And then the plot thickens: We're often advised to go against our conditioning, to become more assertive and ask for what we deserve. But it turns out that, while negotiating may get us what we want, for women, it also comes at a cost.

Researchers found that women who did negotiate were more likely to be treated poorly than their male peers. Why? Because society has deeply ingrained expectations of how women and men are "supposed" to behave.[9] As a Harvard Law School report states, "Relative to men who ask for more, women are penalized financially, are considered less hirable and less likable, and are less likely to be promoted."[10] Further, in a number of studies, researchers asked participants to note their impressions of employees who negotiate their salaries, versus those who don't. Then, they compared employers' willingness to collaborate with the employee after that negotiation. If employers were less interested in working with the employee after they negotiated, that reticence was considered a "social cost" of negotiation. Studies have shown that women experience a higher social cost of negotiating their pay than their male peers—significantly so.[11] Our hesitance to ask for more is very much based in reality.

Unfortunately, the backlash women encounter is hard to combat, particularly because people don't recognize their bias. As Dartmouth business professor Jennifer Dannals explains, "Most of the people are not going into these negotiations thinking explicitly, 'I really hate when women are more assertive.'"[12]

But researchers identified an interesting twist: "We love it when women negotiate assertively for *others*. It's just when women are negotiating assertively for *themselves*—particularly around pay—where we find backlash."[13] That means there's something we can do to shift the stakes, incurring less of that social cost. Harvard Kennedy School professor and chair of the school's Management, Leadership, and Decision Sciences Area Hannah Riley Bowles recommends that you use a "relational account." She describes that as "asking for what you want while signaling to your negotiating counterpart that you are also taking their perspective."[14] How do you do that?

Start by explaining why it makes sense—from their perspective—for you to negotiate in this context. For example, when Sheryl Sandberg was negotiating with Facebook, she said, "Of course, you realize that you're hiring me to run your deal team so you want me to be a good negotiator."[15] She was highlighting the fact that being a good negotiator was core to the role for which she was being considered, so it made sense for her to negotiate during the hiring process.

What if you haven't quite reached Sandberg status? Bowles found that the following line was effective for someone more junior: "I don't know how typical it is for people at my level to negotiate, but I'm hopeful that you'll see my skills at negotiating as something important that I can bring to the job."[16]

Bowles found that people were more likely to agree to the request when context was provided, versus when candidates asked for greater compensation without providing an explanation. Demonstrating an awareness of and concern for the organization made a major difference. In fact, Bowles and her team found no significant difference in social cost incurred between those who used a relational account and those who passed on negotiating altogether!

Bowles acknowledged that the need to invoke concern for organizational relationships is incredibly frustrating to many women, and rightfully so. But if pragmatism is the goal, this is an effective strategy. And, as she notes, "It is good advice for *any* negotiator—male or female—to ask for what they want in terms that their counterparts will perceive as legitimate and mutually beneficial."[17]

Prodding the Equity Problem

As we've discussed, the pay gap isn't just tied to gender. For example, college-educated Black men earn about 80 percent of what college-educated white men earn. Hispanic women earn just 62.2 percent of what their white male counterparts earn. And while Asian women earn 95.8 percent of what white men do, they took home only 78.3 percent of what Asian men did in 2016.[18]

How does race affect negotiations? Professor Morela Hernandez conducted a study to find out. She and her team assigned 144 people of different races to play the role of candidate or hiring evaluator in a simulation. After negotiating, participants answered questions to uncover racial bias. She and her team found that Black and white candidates were just as likely to negotiate their salaries. But evaluators who scored high on racial bias thought Black candidates negotiated more often than white candidates. "This false perception, likely based on the biased evaluators' expectation that Black candidates would and should settle for less, led them to penalize Black candidates for negotiating by granting fewer salary concessions."[19] Further, Professor Hernandez and her team found that whenever Black candidates made an offer or countered the offers they were given, those who scored high on racial bias gave them an average of $300 less. On the other hand, those with low racial bias scores were more accurate in their perception of negotiating frequency and were more equitable in the offers they made.[20]

Multiple studies have demonstrated the compounding effects of multiple disenfranchised identities. For example, Yale's Ian Ayres conducted a famous study in 1995 that demonstrated that car dealers made much higher opening offers to Black and female participants than they did to white men.[21] Those opening offers ultimately affected how much each group paid: "Average dealer profit was $362 from white men, $504 from white women, $783 from Black men, and $1,237 from Black women. This was true despite the fact that participants were trained in advance to negotiate the same way."[22]

In negotiations, bias is often compounded by our own cultural expectations. Researchers Deepa Purushothaman, Deborah M. Kolb, Hannah Riley Bowles, and Valerie Purdie-Greenaway interviewed more than one thousand professional and executive women of color on negotiations. They found that most were hesitant to negotiate due to cultural norms. "Black women found that revealing ambitious intentions and a healthy self-esteem caused them to be misinterpreted as angry, difficult, or aggressive. Many Asian cultures teach a reverence for authority that creates expectations with themselves and others that they should conform. Many immigrant Latinas are cautioned based on family experience not to rock the boat and are taught to keep their heads down."[23]

The participants also ran into challenges with the concept of negotiation itself, which is often viewed as "formal bargaining [typically] associated with white male norms. It also overshadows everyday opportunities for [women of color] to get what they need and want at work"[24]

Further, many of the interviewees felt the advice white women often receive—advice like "lean in" or "just say no"—didn't really apply to them.[25] (As I mentioned, so often, we're already all the way leaned in!)

The women faced numerous mixed messages, which added to the challenge. For example, they were constantly upheld as the exception and thus were met with higher expectations on their performance, all while facing pressure to conform.

But all hope is not lost. Based on their interviews and more than two decades of research, Purushothaman, Kolb, Bowles, and Purdie-Greenaway identified negotiation strategies to help navigate the unique challenges people of multiple disenfranchised identities face when it comes to negotiations.

The "Yes, and" Strategy

So often, we're asked to take on work that is not actually part of our job description. Chairing the Diversity, Equity, and Inclusion Committee, or recruiting, or shouldering part of the workload for a colleague who isn't quite pulling their weight. One tactic is to treat every additional request as an opportunity for negotiation. Professor Deborah M. Kolb explained that Howard Raiffa had once advised her, "Don't say 'no,' ask yourself at what price you would take the job."[26]

"Yes, and" is her take on that approach, one tailored to the unique challenges women face: "In addition to being expected to do more invisible work without credit, a woman is also more likely to suffer from backlash if she refuses. People may like her less and are more likely to describe her as difficult and selfish."[27] Professor Kolb's "yes, and" preempts those reactions. "The 'yes' demonstrates that you take the request seriously, that you care about the relationship and are committed to the organization. The 'and' makes you and the person doing the asking consider what it would take to make the ask work in practice ... The 'and' becomes the basis for the negotiation where you try to figure out what would make the 'ask' work."[28]

For example, if your boss asks you to lead a new initiative on top of your current workload, instead of simply declining, you might say, "**Yes,** I'm excited about leading this initiative, **and** to make it successful I would need to shift some of my current responsibilities to someone else during this period," or "Yes, I'd be happy to take this on, and I'll need additional resources or an adjusted timeline for my other projects." The "and" creates space for a productive discussion about what support, resources, time allocation, or compensation might be necessary to make accepting the additional work feasible and beneficial for both parties.

If they're not willing to accommodate you, you have important information about the kind of environment you're in—and the option to move on.

Share the Load

When we're one of the "only ones" in our organizations, we often find ourselves handling more administrative tasks than our peers. If you've noticed that you're bearing the brunt of those responsibilities—or even just handling more than your colleagues—you could talk to your team about sharing the load. Particularly since the work you're being asked to take on benefits the whole team. Making the shift can be tricky, as it requires their buy-in. However, getting it can be transformational not only for your experience, but for the culture as a whole. And don't be afraid to lean on your manager for support; the Women in the Workplace study found that those who ask their managers for advice on how to move up in their organizations are more likely to get raises. That's particularly vital when you consider that managers are less likely to volunteer that kind of support on their own.[29]

Keep in mind that this particular strategy is all about trust, a crucial component of effective negotiations. When you engender trust—with your team; your board; a future employer; potential co-founder; anyone, really—you're that much closer to arriving at an outcome that will satisfy you both.

Weigh Your Options

What if you see real value in an initiative your board, supervisors, or peers seem to find less pressing? Purushothaman, Kolb, Bowles, and Purdie-

Greenaway recommend considering your options. You could let it go, determining that you're willing to stay focused on their priorities and put yours aside. You could make your case, asking for a pilot or trial to test your idea in the real world. Or you could see what other organizations have to offer, looking for other opportunities, and even using potential offers to renegotiate your role with your current company.[30]

As they so beautifully articulate, "Negotiation is a tool for asking for what you want and deserve, bending norms to break open new paths, and shaping new ways of working."[31] True negotiation helps all parties arrive at a better situation or solution. You get what you need to do your best work, and they understand what it takes to get the job done. Wins all around!

Additionally, remembering that you have options can keep you from settling for something that isn't worth your time, treasure, or talent—all of which are extremely valuable.

The Benefits of Pay Transparency

There's more good news: Societal shifts are making it easier to make your case, particularly when it comes to compensation. For years, websites like Glassdoor.com have been moving the needle on pay transparency, helping to open up conversations about what people actually make in specific roles and industries. Recent legislative moves to promote pay transparency in various states serve to reduce the pay gap. In September of 2023, New York enacted a pay transparency law requiring many employers to include a salary range in job postings. California, Colorado, and Washington have passed similar laws, with more states looking to follow suit. Some states have made it illegal to ask about salary history to help combat the pay gap. Others have addressed gender inequity directly, with laws like the Massachusetts Equal Pay Act, which states that employees cannot be paid less than colleagues of a different gender for similar work.

The push for transparency is making an impact not just on our laws, but also on our culture. In August of 2023, half of online job listings included salary ranges, compared to just 18.4 percent of listings in February of 2020.[32] As Indiana University Kelley School of Business Associate Professor of Management Tomasz Obloj and University of Utah Eccles School of Business Presidential Professor of Strategy and Strategic Leadership Todd Zenger explain, "With the growth of such pay transparency, the lingering norms and policies around pay secrecy have simply lost their teeth."[33]

Knowing who you are, what you're worth, and how to make your case can go a long way.

That's great news when it comes to reducing pay inequity across various dimensions of identity—gender, ethnicity, sexual orientation, and more.[34] For example, Obloj and Zenger's study, "The Influence of Pay Transparency on (Gender) Inequity, Inequality, and the Performance Basis of Pay," found that pay transparency had significantly reduced the gender pay gap at academic institutions—and, in some cases, eliminated it entirely.[35]

With that said, pay transparency creates additional complications. Obloj and Zenger's study "suggests that while pay transparency brings more equitable pay—pay that is more consistently linked to performance across employees—it also results in pay that is flatter, more equal, and less performance based."[36] In other words, because pay has been made so public, employees have less leverage when it comes to making a case for themselves. That may mean you've still got your work cut out for you when it comes to making your case.

Knowing who you are, what you're worth, and how to make your case can go a long way. But if you're stuck, don't hesitate to reach out to your personal board of directors—especially those who have been there and done that.

Consult Your Crew

I remember the day Em shared their negotiations struggles. Em was a first-time CEO, young and bright, with an incredible future ahead of them. We had met through mutual friends and struck up a mentoring relationship of sorts. They would check every so often, updating me on their company's progress and asking questions as things evolved.

When I ran into them at a friend's event, I was thrilled to see them.

"How's everything going?" I asked.

Em got teary-eyed and looked down at their hands. I could tell they weren't doing well.

"What's going on?" I asked, placing a careful hand on their shoulder.

"Well, everything's going really well with the company. We've hit or exceeded all of our benchmarks. We've completed several rounds of financing. We've got plenty of money in the bank. But I've been trying to negotiate an increase in my salary—just to the fiftieth percentile—and the board isn't having it."

"Where does your compensation fall right now?" I asked.

"The twenty-fifth percentile," they responded.

I'd helped them hire, manage, and negotiate some of their executives' salaries. I knew that many of the executives were paid quite well, clocking in at the fiftieth percentile—if not higher. In fact, compensating the executive team fairly was supposedly part of the board's philosophy. Em, it seemed, was an exception to that rule. They were being significantly underpaid. And this was their company! They were the chief executive and had been working 24/7 to bring the vision to life.

Whenever Em brought up their salary, the board made them feel bad about themself, insinuating that they were being inappropriate or greedy for asking for what they deserved. Fortunately, they had negotiated well regarding their equity and control of the board. I was really proud of them for that!

I listened to everything they said and reinforced their perspective. Of course Em should be paid what they deserve. Further, what kind of message was this sending to their executive team and to the organization at large?

I decided to bring in reinforcements. With their permission, I connected with a number of other people Em trusted, other professionals with relevant experience—attorneys, compensation consultants, leaders in their industry—and let them know what was happening. These mirrors reflected back valuable perspectives Em couldn't see alone; they shared their experiences with negotiation: the good, the bad, and the ugly, and how they got through. Each person's story acted as a different mirror, showing Em various angles of the situation and possible paths forward. Together, we created a circle of mirrors that gave Em a complete view of their options and coached them on how to handle the next set of conversations.

The night after Em spoke with their board, I called to check in. "How'd it go, Em?" I asked.

They paused and swallowed. "Not well. A board member cut me off while I was trying to make my case. She said she was surprised by me, that the conversation was making her lose confidence in me."

That was pretty disappointing to hear. But I'd seen things unfold similarly many times. "You're being gaslit," I told them, explaining what the term meant. At that moment, a lightbulb went off.

"Oh my gosh, I *am* being gaslit!" they responded. "I can't believe how bad they've made me feel for asking for the basics."

But because they had negotiated well when it came to their board and their equity, we had a way to move forward. "This is your company, and it's in your best interest to find board members who will support you and your vision," I told them. We worked on a plan for them to change the composition of their board, which they had the power to do, and they followed through.

Finding the right people for their board changed everything. They were able to move forward in all ways with less pushback and were finally being compensated fairly.

During one of our check-ins, Em told me that convening a personal board of directors made all the difference. "Everyone's stories and advice helped so much," they shared. "They gave me the confidence and courage to advocate for myself."

Do Your Homework

As you know by now, a personal board of directors can be an invaluable resource. But what else can you do to set yourself up for success in negotiation? Do your homework. Knowing what you want, what else is out there, and how it compares to the offer in front of you can go a long way.

Take some time to consider your desired outcome. What's your ideal scenario here?

Once you've gotten clear on that, it's time to think about where the other party is coming from, and what a win would look like for them. When you understand both sides of the coin, you're well positioned to find the win-win. Can you imagine getting to a place where everyone's happy? What does it look like?

But before you get too deep into that vision of utopia, consider your non-negotiables. What *won't* you compromise on? Identifying non-negotiables up front is crucial to your success, as it sets you up to make compromises and concessions that you can still feel good about at the end of the day.

By the same token, how can you empower your counterparts to concede? Is there something beneficial you could provide that would make them more likely to give you what you want? Or is it simply a matter of articulating exactly why your approach makes sense, with a clear explanation of how it will benefit the business?

Now, consider the key players. To identify who you need to win over, look at the organizational chart, but also pay attention to informal power dynamics. Who gets deferred to in meetings? Whose opinions seem to carry the most weight in decision-making? Ask trusted colleagues about who truly influences outcomes in your organization. Is it the board chair, the CEO, the CFO? Research their backgrounds and previous positions to understand their decision-making patterns. Look for clues in company communications about their priorities and what they value most. What do you think they want to see, specifically? Understanding both their professional objectives and personal motivations will help you anticipate what they might be willing to concede and what they'll hold firm on during negotiations. What would they, as an individual, need to concede?

As you consider your negotiation counterparts, think about whether or not *you're* the right person to handle the negotiation. Maybe someone else in your company is better suited for the conversation, or maybe you need to rally external troops—like bankers, attorneys, or subject-matter experts—who can be more effective.

It's worth considering whether or not you're the right party to handle the negotiations *even* when you're negotiating your own compensation. Maybe you're better off working through a potential supervisor who's invested in bringing you on, or through a recruiter, or another board member—especially if you struggle to advocate for yourself, as so many of us do.

Having a different party do the asking can shift your counterpart's perspective entirely and significantly increase the chance that you'll be successful. Sometimes, a little mansplaining can go a long way. For example, a woman founder I know said one of her fundraising strategies is to bring a tall white man along for those money conversations. And I know plenty of women who thwart the prospect of paying a premium for their car due to gender and race—a very real concern, as the research shows—by bringing along a male companion.

Then, think about your strategy. If you're negotiating, what style feels authentic to you? What kind of approach has the potential to make a difference? Maybe you rely on explaining how your asks will benefit them. Perhaps you lean on Professor Kolb's "yes, and" strategy, explaining exactly what it will take to arrive at a win-win. Or maybe you find a way that's unique to you, drawing on your strengths and unique talents to demonstrate the value of your proposal.

Now, what about the details? You may want to ask for more than you actually expect to get, knowing that they'll likely counter. Or if you're doing the offering, you may want to start with a smaller number, knowing your counterpart is likely to ask for more. On the other hand, if you don't want to play any games, let them know, asserting that this is your best and final offer, and they can take it or leave it. All of the work you've done to date to know what you want, what they're looking for, what a win-win looks like, and more should inform this approach.

Once you've landed on your strategy, take the time to get into the right headspace. Strike a power pose in your living room before you leave for the meeting. Raise your arms above your head in the car once you park, or take a wide stance in the bathroom stall right before you head into the boardroom. Do what you need to do to shift your internal chemistry and raise your vibration so your head's in the game. You are powerful beyond measure. Your presence should reflect that.

When you go into it, be kind. The goal isn't to strip the other person of their power or make them lose faith in their own prowess. It's to land somewhere you can both live with. Someone once told me that the best deals are ones where everyone's a little unhappy. Handling negotiations gracefully helps establish and maintain relationships that will serve you throughout your career, no matter how this particular conversation goes.

And finally, be authentic. Many of the tactics that serve those who have long been part of the business majority won't serve you, and attempting to emulate their behavior will likely read as false. You don't have to put on a poker face if you've never been able to hold one before, for instance. There's a lot of value in being honest, forthright, passionate, and empathetic—and embodying those remarkable qualities doesn't mean you have to lose sight of what you're negotiating for. Move forward in a manner that's congruent with your communication style, your leadership style, and your values, and you'll be well positioned for success. Note, too, that if things don't turn out the way you want, that's important information. You get to choose how to proceed, and one of those choices may be walking away.

Ultimately, you have to live with the outcome—and yourself. If you can walk away feeling good about both, I'd say the negotiation was a success.

Step into Your Power

- **Consider your options.** Get familiar with any offer you've got and how it compares to your current role or resources. Also research the standard for your role or industry. Knowing these things puts you in a good position to make your case. For example, if you know the typical salary range for a particular role, you have the information you need to better advocate for yourself.

- **See the big picture.** If you're considering a job offer, it's important to recognize that compensation is bigger than salary alone. Weigh the benefits and materials being offered to you (think tech or a stipend to set up your home office) alongside the amount of pay you'll take home.

- **Keep it comfortable.** Pay equity expert and founder of Equal Pay Negotiations Katie Donovan recommends negotiating in a manner that feels most comfortable to you. That may mean saving your salary request for an email rather than dropping it in the room, or talking details over text rather than on the phone. If it works for you, work it to get what you need.

- **Explain what's in it for them.** It may be a hard pill to swallow, but society hasn't set us up for success in the negotiations department. With that in mind—and with the understanding that thinking about the good of the organization is good for *everyone*—think about how you can make your case in a way that takes your counterpart's perspective into account.

We've talked about how to understand yourself and your environment, and how to put the puzzle pieces together, leveraging that knowledge to drive the outcomes you want. You know what you bring to the table, what you'll find there, and how to capture the attention of those seated around you. Now, it's time to think about something a little less tangible but just as vital as everything we've covered, if not more so: your energy.

CHAPTER 11

HARNESS YOUR PRESENCE
Managing Your Energy to Level Up

**"Take a stand.
Be known for your courage and confidence."**

–Indra Nooyi

remember how my energy shifted when I finally settled into my power. I had gotten clear about my values and why I was doing the things that I did, often for the betterment of my team or company at large. The nervousness that used to thrum beneath my skin had transformed into a quiet confidence. For the first time in a really long time, it felt good to be me.

Then something interesting happened. I noticed that the people around me began to react differently to my presence too. I realized I could influence my interactions and even the dynamics of a room. When I relaxed, others seemed to relax alongside me. Tense conversations seemed to transition into constructive dialogue. Conversations about big problems transformed into data-seeking discussions about the opportunities in front of us. The whole vibe shifted shortly after I walked through the door.

What changed?

I had been focused on cultivating my spiritual practice, and along the way I found my authentic self: someone a lot easier going than I had thought. I'd been contorting myself to fit others' perceptions of me—and

199

my perceptions of a leader—so much so that I'd forgotten my true nature. As it turned out, I wasn't a type A after all. I'd only been playing one in the office because I thought that's what I needed to do to get ahead. When I embraced my authentic self and the energy that came with it, I let go of the need to prove myself and my credibility. I found peace and power, and so did those around me.

> **When you're in a position of power, your internal environment—what you feel on the inside—is reflected in your external environment, in the experience of those around you.**

That became even more apparent as I took on more responsibility, stepping into higher-level leadership positions. I could imbue a space with the calmness, openness, and sense of safety that I felt at my core. And that energy helped everyone I worked with accomplish incredible things. It was a testament to an important truth: **When you're in a position of power, your internal environment—what you feel on the inside—is reflected in your external environment, in the experience of those around you.** And, as you may have heard from a certain caped guy in tights, with great power comes great responsibility.

When you become CEO, you're no longer a content or category expert. You're not driving any particular part of the organization. Instead, you're there to enable others to step into *their* power, to catalyze their ability to drive progress. I realized that my job was to hold space to create a safe environment; to house excellence and innovation.

But all of us, at every phase and stage of our lives and careers, have the ability to change our reality by managing our energy, to be centered; powerful; confident, and yes, fly over the bullshit, above the pull of FIDS. It's that energetic alignment, the integration of who you are and what you do, that truly enables you to tap into your power and live your best life.

It took me years to realize that was the reason why, when I was at McKinsey, "presence" was among our vital hiring criteria. So many of us were younger and less experienced than the executives we were advising. In so many cases, we had to exert influence without authority. It's presence, or energy, that makes that possible.

When you show up with confidence—really, truly believing in your-self and what you're there to do—that means you show up calm, centered, and aligned. And as a result, you command respect.

Create Alignment

You've probably heard powerful quotes from influential leaders across time and space that speak to the importance of your presence: Mahatma Gandhi said, "Be the change you wish to see in the world." Self-development author and speaker Wayne Dyer wrote a book titled *Change Your Thoughts—Change Your Life*, which describes the power of align-ing how you think with how you want to live. That requires you to determine your priorities, at this stage in the game and in life at large, and make sure you are acting accordingly. As Tony Robbins explains, where focus goes, energy flows. And if you don't take the time to focus on what matters, then you're living a life of someone else's design.

What do you want to prioritize as you design your life? Is it your work, family, or friends? Exploring the world or investing in your future? With that in mind, what compromises are you willing to make? Will you give up time with your spouse or your kids to launch your dream com-pany? Or, on the flipside, are you ready to sacrifice quick professional progress to be there for the milestones in your children's lives? Note that the decisions you make don't have to be forever, but they must serve the priorities you're interested in pursuing right now. Personally, I'm leaning into life at home at the moment, as I know I only have my children here for the next few years, before they leave for college. I don't want to miss out on that. It's a personal decision, and one I'm proud to make. And it's not necessarily the same one I made at other phases of my life and career, or one I'll make in the future.

Compromise also means letting go of perfection. That may be hard to accept; I know it was for me! But when you let go of others' expectations, and even some of the unrealistic expectations you have for yourself, you reduce your stress and thus have more energy to spend on the things that matter.

My swami and guru used to talk about intelligent living, which he defined as accepting things as they are and letting go of perfection. Reality is reality. The situation is what it is, the facts are what they are. It's only when we can't accept them that we find ourselves in an energy-draining fight where we can't help but lose. After all, it's a battle against ourselves.

To live intentionally, you must be willing to embrace compromise, to let go of the junk that will prevent you from thriving. There are only so many hours in a day. If you want to make time to attend your kid's soccer game, or to practice pottery, or to keep a weekly date night with your spouse, or anything else that matters to you, you're going to have to give up some of the other stuff. You may have to send that report out the door without proofing it three extra times, or trust someone else to finalize the details while you make your way to the field. You may have to skip out on certain evening commitments to make others work or otherwise allocate the limited time and resources you have.

When you know what your priorities are, it becomes easy to let go of the other stuff. If you're unsure about whether a particular opportunity aligns, check in with yourself. Is this how you want to be spending your time?

You can ask yourself how someone makes you feel; a potential supervisor or board member, for example. Do you want to talk to this person? Can you imagine what it might feel like to communicate with them on a daily basis? When you interact with them, do they bring your energy level down, or invigorate you, inspiring you to level up and meet the challenge ahead? When a professional opportunity presents itself, does it make you feel excited? Or is there a sense of dread there, lurking behind what seems to be a major boon to your career?

You can gut-check the simple stuff, too: How do you respond internally when a friend calls and asks you to dinner? Is it a "Hell yes," or does the outing feel like yet another chore on an endless to-do list?

Energy management is a practice, as you'll see, but it's also a gauge. On a gut level, you know what's right for you. I'm a major proponent of "JOMO": the Joy of Missing Out, FOMO's serene, self-actualized cousin. There's immense pleasure to be found in skipping the stuff that isn't meant for you. It's often just a matter of listening to the inner voice that's been there all along. That's a way of life—and it's a lifelong journey, and I'm still working on it after a lifetime of overextending myself!

To stay on track, I've got a mantra that helps me remember what matters to me: *Every day counts, every day counts, every day counts.* Because I lost my dad at such a young age, I'm intimately familiar with the fact that I can't take things for granted. Today is a blessing, and tomorrow isn't promised. Life is too short not to listen to that inner voice. Figure out how you want to live and then commit. Take the best and drop the rest. Every day counts. Know, too, that your priorities will change, and to maintain alignment, you've got to keep reassessing them. That's part of the gig.

What does alignment feel like? I'd describe it as ten-out-of-ten energy. You're totally thriving. You're doing what you love and loving what you do, and as a result you're inspired by tomorrow's potential and content with things today. You love your job and your life, and that sense of satisfaction is palpable to others. That kind of energy is infectious, and being around someone with ten-out-of-ten energy is the opposite of standing near someone whose energy is frenetic or scattered.

Once you find alignment, it's time to calibrate your daily thoughts and actions, not only checking your priorities but keeping yourself in a state of flow.

Find Your Flow

We don't often get a lot of slack, especially early in our careers. With so many people being so quick to write us off, we've got to put our best foot forward in any given moment, at any given meeting, on any given day. That often means doing the work to achieve and return to a state of "flow," an embodiment of the alignment between who we are and what we do, multiple times throughout the day. Psychologist "Mihály Csíkszentmihályi coined the term in the 1960s, while studying the creative process.[1] We often find flow when we're completely caught up in an activity: making art, reading, writing, working out, tackling a math problem or spreadsheet. We're entirely focused on the task at hand, and as a result, time seems to slip away. We melt into what we're doing and often find the best version of ourselves and our work as a result.

The path to flow looks different for everyone. For me, it's meditation, finding a quiet space to close my eyes, breathe, and clear my mind so I can collect my thoughts and move forward. For you it may be exercise, arriving at flow drenched in sweat at level ten on the treadmill, focusing on minuscule muscles in a Pilates class, or even taking the time to drop into a quick set of pushups behind your desk to get into the right headspace when you can't hit the gym. For others, it may be saying affirmations while staring into the mirror. Still others might find flow by listening to music, letting their heartbeat sync to the rhythm, or dancing with all they've got until their body seems to meld with the sound. The point is to get back to clarity: an internal place where you know who you are, what you want to do, and what's driving you.

Take the time to check in with yourself throughout the day. If you notice that you're feeling less than your best, do what you need to do to get back into flow.

But what about the stuff that doesn't feel especially inspiring? The small, tedious tasks that are part of the game of life?

You can find a way to tap into flow there, too. My kids are charged with doing the dishes in our house, and they take turns choosing the music to get them through. Suddenly, the beat hits and something that's potentially painful feels light and fun, quickly transforming into a family bonding session where we're all in our groove. Before we know it, those dishes are sparkling and sitting on the rack, and we're all feeling better than we were before taking on the task.

But what about when you're feeling overwhelmed or even panicked? I'm talking about those moments when meditation or even small tasks feel like too much to bear.

Regulate Your Nervous System

When your heart starts racing, your palms begin sweating, or your mind goes blank just when you need clarity most? These are telltale signs of a dysregulated nervous system—and they can sabotage your leadership presence in critical moments.

Our bodies weren't designed for the constant vigilance that modern leadership demands. When I was preparing for major investor presentations as CEO or difficult board conversations, I found myself unable to sleep through the nights. My thoughts raced, my breathing was shallow, and despite knowing my material cold, it was difficult to access that knowledge during challenging situations. My nervous system was hijacked by stress.

But you can combat this by getting back to basics—tapping into your physical self to find calm when it's most critical.

Here are five concrete practices I've found to be transformative:

1. **The ninety-second reset:** Before entering any high-stakes situation, find a private space and take a deep breath, counting to four as you inhale through your nose, holding for seven counts, and exhaling slowly through your mouth for eight counts. Do this three times total. This practice immediately activates your parasympathetic nervous system, lowering stress hormones within ninety seconds. I've done it in bathroom stalls before board meetings, and it works.

2. **Hand on heart:** When you feel anxiety rising during a meeting, discreetly place one hand on your heart while continuing the conversation. This simple physical anchor sends safety signals to your brain and helps you stay present.

3. **Cold water splash:** Keep a cold water bottle with you. When stress mounts, excuse yourself briefly, go to the restroom, and splash cold water on your wrists or press the cold bottle against the back of your neck. The temperature change triggers an immediate physiological shift out of fight-or-flight mode.

4. **Schedule recovery blocks:** In your calendar, block twenty-minute "recovery zones" between high-intensity meetings. Use this time to walk outside, stretch, or simply sit quietly. One tech executive I mentor sets a non-negotiable fifteen-minute buffer after board meetings where she does nothing but breathe and integrate before moving to her next commitment.

5. **Evening wind-down ritual:** Create a consistent ten-minute routine that signals to your body it's time to shift from performance mode to recovery. This might include turning off screens, gentle stretching, or writing down tomorrow's priorities so your brain can stop rehearsing them. This boundary between work and rest is critical for nervous system regulation.

These practices aren't luxuries, they're essential leadership tools. When your nervous system is regulated, you access your full intelligence, creativity, and relational capacity. You become immune to emotional contagion in tense situations. You make decisions from clarity rather than fear. And crucially, you model this centered presence for your team, creating a ripple effect throughout your organization.

Heed the Signals

Remember that no one can be at a ten out of ten all the time, particularly when culture and society have taught you to please others first and foremost. To be of service as a spouse, child, and parent. To pick up the slack, fill in the blanks, and make sure nothing's ever dropped, doing whatever it takes to get the job done.

In Indian culture, we have a duty to take care of others around us. In the Vedic tradition, we're urged to be a contributor, not a consumer; a giver, not a grabber. That's ingrained in us from the time we're children, and it's quite important to the fabric of society. It's why we so often ask high-powered women, "How do you do it all?" Most of us have learned the hard way that there's no such thing as work-life balance. There is just prioritization. So much of our lives are work, and work that we do in service of others. But that doesn't necessarily serve us in the boardroom, where others are there to push their own agendas and bypass anyone who gets in their way.

Further, life is full of obstacles and curveballs. Successfully managing our energy is also about our ability to be resilient, to meet the challenges that arise and to grow from them. If you're feeling upset by a particular circumstance, it's a good indication that something from your past is bubbling up, and that it may be time to finally deal with it so you can get back to that flow state. The universe gives us ample opportunity to learn crucial lessons, providing situation after situation to urge us to action. It's up to you to pick up on the shifts in your energy and take the time to course correct.

When your reserves get low, that's another signal to adjust. You can't possibly serve yourself or others well in that condition. It's not responsible or productive to keep driving yourself into the ground. Quite simply, if you're working around the clock at home or in the office and ignoring your physical and mental health in the process, there's no way to be the best leader, parent, spouse, or friend you can be. That's the time to recalibrate, to do what you need to do to get back to where you want to be. You've probably heard the rule on airplanes and in life: You've got to put your oxygen mask on first if you want to be of any help to others.

To lean on another metaphor, when we're racing toward an end goal, we often forget that life *is* the journey to get there. That we can find health, happiness, and freedom on our way to the biggest achievements. We fail to realize that if we don't take the time to do that, we're actually lost. If you're feeling drained spiritually, physically, emotionally, or mentally, this is your sign to hit pause and (another metaphor incoming) fill your cup. You've got to invest in self-care.

Invest in Self-Care

Let's pause for a minute. What did you think when you just read "self-care"?

Maybe you tried to think about the last time you did something nice for yourself, wracking your brain for evidence of you doing right by you. Maybe you shook your head, picturing what so many have presented as a half-hearted solution to society's shortcomings: a mani-pedi as a means of escaping a toxic work environment or running on caffeine until you can switch to a big glass of wine at the end of the day. That's not what I'm talking about.

This is real deal self-care, the kind that prevents us from being inauthentic, disingenuous, and incongruent so that we can find and live by our values and embody our truest sense of self. Don't get me wrong: That's a whole lot easier said than done. It's why those mani-pedis and bevy of beverages are so appealing in the first place.

Like so many overachievers, for so long, I was dead set on trying to belong, to prove myself, to make it. It was a painful existence. But more than the external hurdles I had to leap, much of the discomfort I was experiencing was coming from not accepting myself—from that lack of energetic alignment. Leaning into self-acceptance and self-love is the first step in taking proper care of yourself. It's also one of the greatest.

True self-care allows you to be a whole person, one who's clear about their mission, vision, values, and the people surrounding them. What does that look like for you? It varies for everyone, but here's what substantive self-care often includes:

- **Setting healthy boundaries:** Learn to say no to demands that drain your energy without providing value. This might mean declining additional work when you're at capacity, limiting time with energy-depleting people, or being clear about when you're available and when you're not.

- **Creating space for solitude:** Make time to be alone with your thoughts. This could be a daily meditation practice, a weekly walk in nature, or even just fifteen minutes of quiet reflection at the beginning or end of each day.

- **Prioritizing physical well-being:** Exercise regularly in ways that energize rather than deplete you. Nourish your body with foods that make you feel good. Sleep enough that you wake feeling rested. And yes, see healthcare providers when needed: Don't put off medical care because you're "too busy."

- **Embracing true rest:** As the Nap Ministry's Tricia Hersey wisely teaches us, rest is resistance in a culture that glorifies overwork. Schedule downtime as though it's as important as any meeting—because it is. True rest might look like napping, sitting quietly without a screen, or simply doing nothing at all.

- **Asking for help:** Delegate tasks both at work and at home. Share the mental load with partners, colleagues, and support systems. Remember that asking for help isn't weakness; it's wisdom.

- **Disengaging from toxic relationships:** Assess which relationships deplete rather than nourish you and create distance where possible. Sometimes the most caring thing you can do for yourself is to step away from people who consistently undermine your well-being.

- **Cultivating pleasure:** Make time for activities that bring you joy—whether that's sexual pleasure, creative expression, or simply indulging in experiences that delight your senses.
- **Pursuing interests outside of work:** Develop hobbies and interests that have nothing to do with your career or productivity. These passions will remind you that your worth isn't tied to what you accomplish.

This kind of comprehensive self-care creates the foundation that allows you to show up fully in your power. When you're depleted, disconnected from your needs, or running on fumes, it's nearly impossible to tap into the energy required to lead effectively and authentically.

The beauty of this approach to self-care is that it becomes a positive feedback loop: When you attend to your needs at this deeper level, you build a greater capacity for clarity, confidence, and a powerful presence in all aspects of your life. You become a mirror reflecting wholeness and balance to those around you—modeling what it looks like to lead from a place of genuine self-regard.

That's what you've got to figure out. Not just moments of indulgence, but a consistent practice of honoring your whole self.

Step into Your Power—Literally

It's one thing to be in alignment, to cultivate and care for yourself so you can stay there. But what happens when you've got a big challenge in front of you? How do you rise to meet it? You've got to build on that alignment, remaining clear on who you are and what you're there to do, all while understanding the spaces you're in and adjusting your energy accordingly to achieve the outcomes you want. If we can flip the switch on our energy as needed and manage it for the better, we can do the same for our lives. Let's talk about how to do just that.

You can raise your vibration to tackle whatever lies ahead, reaffirming your confidence in your ability to thrive. Making that adjustment is necessary for all of us from time to time. As much as we wish it weren't the case, we're all susceptible to nerves and intimidation from time to time.

Even Rebecca Welton, the rich and powerful fictional football club owner on *Ted Lasso*, struggled to manage her energy and show up as her best self when she first took over AFC Richmond. In one scene, before a big meeting, she takes a moment to look in the mirror, take a deep breath, and gather the energy from the floor, taking on a power pose reminiscent of kickass Hindu goddess Kali.

The goddess of death, time, and doomsday, Kali is also a symbol of feminine energy, creativity, and fertility. When Rebecca strikes her pose, lifting her arms, opening her mouth wide, and sticking out her tongue, she sees her child-self reflected in the mirror, doing the same. And when she lets the pose go, her shoulders are back, hands poised on her hips. Her adult-self stares back at her. Her face is relaxed, and there's a quiet confidence about her that wasn't there before.[2] She has quite literally stepped into her power. She's ready to rule. And there's data behind that particular move: the power pose.

Science says our mindset follows our actions, not the other way around. Slumping over, looking down, and crossing your arms in front of your chest makes you feel closed off and small. On the flipside, getting expansive has the potential to make you feel like you can take on the world. In 2010, researchers Dana Carney, Amy Cuddy, and Andy Yap published a study titled "Power Posing: Brief Nonverbal Displays Affect Neuroendocrine Levels and Risk Tolerance." That's a lot of words to describe a relatively simple finding: that posing in powerful ways—literally taking up more space, for instance, by adopting a wider stance and spreading your arms above your head for a short stint before a big meeting—affects the way we feel and act, which cause neuroendocrine and behavioral changes in our bodies. In even fewer words, posing powerfully actually makes you more powerful.[3]

How does it work? The study found that power posing increases testosterone, the male sex hormone associated with feelings of power and control, and decreases cortisol—a major stress hormone. The combination of high testosterone and low cortisol is "linked to fearlessness, risk-taking, and insensitivity to punishment."[4] While there's been some debate about whether the study's results were overstated, numerous other findings show that there's definitely something to it. A meta-analytic review of 88 studies with a combined total of 9,799 participants found a few different things. First, and perhaps most significantly, the majority of participants reported "feeling powerful, confident, and positive."[5] Power posing made them *feel* stronger. Behavioral and physiological effects were less reliably replicated. But what you feel matters a great deal.

Tony Robbins, one of the world's best-known life and business strategists, has long promoted the effects of power posing—even before that first study dropped. As he explains, "The way you use your body affects the way your mind works. You can try and get yourself in the right mental state by going, 'I'm happy, I'm happy, I'm happy, I'm happy,' and your brain goes, 'B.S., I'm not happy.' But if you change your body strongly enough, it will [follow suit]."[6]

Tony shares with his audiences what he's taught, " . . . doctors, lawyers, billionaire people, kids, people in prison, some of the great athletes in the world": To stand in a wide stance, with your head up and shoulders back and take big breaths for two minutes to feel the power. But he recommends that you don't stop there. Make a dynamic move that makes you feel strong: pump your fists, stomp your feet, do whatever you need to do to take up space. Next, he suggests pairing all that with the loudest sound you can, a sound that makes you feel unstoppable.[7] Then, notice any changes in how you move, how you feel, and how you act.

While you may not feel comfortable yelling in your loudest voice in the office restroom, go ahead and try striking a pose somewhere private before your next big meeting. To up your sense of power and control, start by moving your body into a shape that reflects that power and control. Take up space. Widen your stance. Spread your arms. Feel a look of quiet confidence come over your face. Chances are you'll feel your energy rise, along with the knowledge that you really are powerful beyond measure.

If you're in need of grounding, there's a hack for that, too. Place your hand on your abdomen and take several deep breaths into your belly. Focus on feeling present and whole. You'll be centered and ready for anything that may come your way, including difficult, emotional conversations.

Read the Room

Note that managing your energy isn't just about commanding attention in any room. It's also about calibrating that energy so you can accomplish what you need to do and feel confident doing it.

I'm always struck by how comfortable I feel when I walk into a room of women or other people of color. I get the sense of what it must feel like to be a straight white man in a typical boardroom, surrounded by peers. When we're in one of those rooms full of mirrors—people with a similar background or sets of experiences—we all tend to give each other the benefit of the doubt. There's not the same pressure to prove how bright and talented we are. Our brilliance—our inherent worth—is assumed. Those striking moments where I'm among peers who look like me serve as a reminder of how I'm still very comfortable with being uncomfortable, even after all these years, and how much discomfort drains our energy. This is how I truly know that **representation matters**.

In a new environment—whether it's a business meeting, a job interview, or a role at a new company—you don't know who's going to be on the other side of the table and how their own biases will inform their impressions of you. That takes a lot out of you, whether you want it to or not. But you do have control over how you show up. When you arrive with internal clarity, you can assess what's coming at you and act accordingly. That may mean showing up a little more forcefully when you sense that the people across from you need to see your strength and understand that you're not a pushover. Maybe they're advocating for something that doesn't jibe with your approach or looking to overstep you on their way to the board. If so, they need to know, for example, that *you* are the CEO of the company, and that anything they want to advance has to go through you. Showing up strong will keep them from questioning you.

Other times, you may have to release your agenda. There are times to plant seeds and let things blossom on their own, softening energetically so your desired outcome can come to fruition. That takes negotiation skills, but also a willingness to let go of what's not serving you—and your expectations.

Still other times, you've got to step back to let others step up. Come off too forcefully in a room full of junior team members and you may intimidate them, inadvertently hindering their willingness to be innovative and share their ideas. It's up to you to regulate that energy to give them space. Fostering psychological safety and helping a less experienced crew step into their power may mean operating at a slightly lower frequency, stepping back a bit to inspire them to be their best. Rather than conveying that you're there to make all the decisions, you're using the cues available to you—verbal and nonverbal alike—to say, "I want the best from *you*."

Keep in mind that finding your place energetically may be more about the phase of life or career that you're in than the room itself. These days, I spend a lot more time listening quietly than I used to. There's less pressure to prove myself, and my energy has shifted to reflect that. When you know why you're there, to be supportive or to lead the charge, you can be the change the room needs to succeed.

If you're unsure, you can always turn to those mirrors for guidance or simply listen for the wise voice in your head—the one that's there to be a source of wisdom, not judgment.

Step into Your Power

Managing your energy may seem more abstract than some of the other strategies we've covered, but it's no less important. In fact, it has an impact on everything you do. Keeping these tips in mind will help you navigate any curveballs thrown your way from a calm, centered place—and determine when it may just be time to move on.

- **Embrace authenticity:** Let go of the need to conform to others' expectations, especially in leadership roles. Authenticity can transform your energy and influence interactions positively.
- **Prioritize and align:** Determine your values and priorities and align your actions accordingly. Focus your energy on what truly matters to you at this stage of your life and career, and don't be afraid to compromise on the rest.
- **Go with the flow:** Regularly check in with yourself throughout the day and adjust your energy with the moves that keep you content and inspired.
- **Invest in self-care:** Ditch the rhetoric about coffee, wine, and mani-pedis. (Unless they bring you joy, of course!) Practice genuine self-care, leaning into self-acceptance and self-love above all else.
- **Calibrate.** Learn to adjust your energy to wield influence in a way that serves your goals. Consider whether you need to do a power pose, centering breathing exercises, or other energetic practices before you walk into a situation.

Well, we're nearing the end of our time together. We've talked about how to understand yourself and your environment, and how to put the puzzle pieces together, leveraging that knowledge to drive the outcomes you want. You know what you bring to the table, what you'll find there, and how to capture the attention of those seated around you. Now that you know what you need to truly level up and thrive, let's talk about what's truly possible in your journey of life.

BE BOLD

Realize Your Dreams

**"Living your best life
is your most important journey in life."**

–Oprah Winfrey

In these pages, you've met a lot of amazing people who have encountered serious hardships personally and professionally—people who have found ways around, through, and over the self-limiting beliefs, challenging relationships, and difficult environments that were holding them back. The last story I want to share is about you.

You were born powerful beyond measure, equipped with the brains and drive and resourcefulness to conquer your wildest dreams. And then somewhere along the way—likely when you were still a child—a person, an environment, your culture, society as a whole, or all of the above, convinced you otherwise.

People made disparaging or dismissive remarks about your intelligence or your talent or simply your difference. They questioned you more than your white, male peers for the sole reason that you didn't fit their vision of a grad student or a lawyer or a doctor or an entrepreneur or an executive. Over the years, those comments added up, and you began to question your worth, your potential, your ambition, or some other quality necessary to make those dreams happen.

Who do I think I am?
Do I deserve to be here?
Maybe I shouldn't really be a board member …
Why don't people believe in me?

In Part I, we confronted the fear, insecurity, doubt, and shame (FIDS) that have kept so many of us playing small. We acknowledged that these feelings aren't just personal shortcomings—they're the result of systemic conditioning that begins in childhood and continues throughout our careers.

I'm here to validate your experience. To assure you that it wasn't all in your head. You were made to feel that way. The conscious and unconscious bias you felt—and likely continue to feel—were very, very real. Women like us have had to wade through many external factors that attempt to limit our power and our effectiveness, being twice as good to get half the credit—all while heeding red flags signaling individual, organizational, and societal toxicity.

Throughout this book, we've journeyed through three essential parts of leadership development for marginalized professionals: knowing yourself, understanding your environment, and setting yourself up for success.

The Journey Within: Knowing Thyself

In Part I, we confronted the **fear, insecurity, doubt, and shame (FIDS) that have kept so many of us playing small. We acknowledged that these feelings aren't just personal shortcomings—they're the result of systemic conditioning that begins in childhood and continues throughout our careers.** We've explored how persistent microaggressions, subtle dismissals, and outright discrimination create an internal landscape where imposter syndrome thrives.

We also identified the four limiting archetypes that so many of us fall into: the People-pleaser, the Imposter, the Bitch Boss, and the Micromanager. These aren't who we truly are, they're roles we've adopted to survive in environments that weren't designed for us. By recognizing these patterns, we gain the power to break through our inner glass ceiling.

The Three Cs—compassion, centering, and celebration—gave us practical tools to reclaim our authentic selves. Self-compassion taught us to treat ourselves with the same kindness we extend to those we love. Centering practices showed us how to return to our core in moments of chaos and uncertainty. And learning to celebrate ourselves—without waiting for external validation—allowed us to acknowledge our own brilliance.

This inner work isn't optional; it's the foundation upon which all external success must be built.

This inner work isn't optional; it's the foundation upon which all external success must be built. When you know who you truly are—powerful beyond measure—no one can shake that knowledge from you. As Marianne Williamson so eloquently stated, "Our deepest fear is not that we are inadequate. Our deepest fear is that we are powerful beyond measure." The realization of this truth is transformative.

Navigating the External: Understanding Your Environment

In Part II, we turned our attention outward, examining the often-challenging environments in which we operate. We identified three common toxic workplaces: fear-based cultures that stifle innovation, cutthroat competitive environments that pit colleagues against each other, and gaslighting cultures that make us question our reality.

We learned to recognize the sophisticated players at the highest levels of organizations: the Tyrants who rule through intimidation, the Rivals who see your success as their failure, and the Deceivers who manipulate reality to maintain control. Understanding that their behavior stems from their own wounds and insecurities allows us to respond with strategic compassion rather than reactive emotion.

We also tackled the thorny issue of perception—how others see us versus how we see ourselves. Whether dealing with misperceptions based purely on bias, assessments that contain kernels of truth, or feedback that's entirely accurate but difficult to hear, we now have frameworks to assess and address these perceptions without losing sight of our authentic selves.

Build a personal board of directors—those essential mirrors who reflect your brilliance back to you when you can't see it yourself.

Most importantly, we established that you deserve a healthy, supportive environment where you can thrive. Organizations like Patagonia, Hilton, and Cisco demonstrate that such places do exist. And if you can't find one, you have the power to create one, just as Imani did with her "No Egos, No Jerks, No Politics" company culture.

The Integration: Setting Yourself Up for Success

In Part III, we brought everything together, providing concrete strategies to leverage your self-knowledge and environmental awareness to create the career and life you desire.

We explored how to **build a personal board of directors—those essential mirrors who reflect your brilliance back to you when you can't see it yourself.** With loyal supporters who have your back, sponsors who advocate for you in rooms you can't access, mentors who guide your growth, role models who inspire your path, and subject-matter experts who fill knowledge gaps, you create a network that amplifies your power.

We tackled the challenge of negotiation, acknowledging the unique barriers that women and other marginalized professionals face when advocating for themselves. Armed with strategies like the "Yes, and" approach and relational accounts, you can now negotiate effectively without triggering backlash or compromising your values.

Finally, we delved into energy management—how to align your inner state with your external presence to command respect and influence outcomes. From power poses that physiologically boost confidence to reading the room and calibrating your energy accordingly, **you now have tools to show up as your most powerful self in any situation.**

The Transformation: From Knowledge to Action

Before we move forward, let's take a moment to reflect on how you got here. Perhaps you kept doing big things, kicking ass, taking names, and flying over bullshit (just as Queen Bey instructed). You continued to make your way in the world, but something changed. As the slights inevitably built up, flying felt harder. Or maybe you haven't even gotten off the ground yet, but the struggles you've had so far make taking flight feel too risky.

> **Transformation requires courage—the courage to dismantle limiting beliefs, to leave toxic environments, to build authentic relationships, to negotiate your worth, and to show up fully in your power.**

Maybe, regardless of where you've gotten, the resistance you've met has made you think smaller than you did as a kid, when you dreamed openly. Maybe that resistance stopped you from dreaming altogether. But something brought you to this book. A colleague, a friend, a loved one, or that little voice inside that knows just how much you can achieve. You wanted to figure out how to step into your power and level up, to run through walls and break the glass ceiling, and to lift others up alongside you. You were ready to claim your seat at the table among senior leaders, decision-makers, and influencers who are helping to shape the world.

The knowledge you've gained through these pages is only valuable when put into action. True **transformation requires courage—the courage to dismantle limiting beliefs, to leave toxic environments, to build authentic relationships, to negotiate your worth, and to show up fully in your power.**

This transformation is much like the metamorphosis of a caterpillar into a butterfly. Scientists have discovered that inside the chrysalis, the caterpillar doesn't simply grow wings—it completely dissolves, breaking down cell by cell until it becomes an undifferentiated soup. From this apparent chaos, those cells reorganize into an entirely new creature capable of flight.

You get to step into your power and decide what you want for yourself, even if it feels scary.

Your journey may feel similarly chaotic at times. You might find yourself questioning everything you thought you knew about yourself and your place in the world. This discomfort isn't a sign that you're doing something wrong; it's evidence that you're undergoing the profound reorganization necessary to emerge in your full power.

The Collective Rise: Lifting as We Climb

When I co-founded the Biotech CEO Sisterhood, I witnessed firsthand the exponential power of women supporting women. What began as a small group has grown to more than 300 female biotech CEOs who lift each other up, share resources, and work to transform an entire industry together. This community has accomplished more collectively than any of us could have achieved alone.

This points to a fundamental truth: Our individual rise contributes to collective progress. Every time you advocate for yourself, you make it easier for someone else to do the same. **Every boundary you set, every negotiation you master, every toxic environment you transform or leave behind … all these actions create ripple effects** that benefit others who share your experiences.

The work you do to recognize your worth and step into your power isn't just for you. It's for every person who has ever felt marginalized, overlooked, or underestimated. It's for the next generation who will inherit the cultures and systems we're transforming. It's for a world that desperately needs the unique contributions only you can make.

Your Turn: Manifesting Your Vision

So what's your story? Not the one others have written for you, but the one you want to author for yourself?

What is the career of your dreams? What kind of life do you want to manifest? What do you want your days to look and feel like?

> Stop right here and write it down. As I mentioned, *The Mirror Effect Workbook & Journal* provides structure to implement everything you've learned in these pages. Through daily reflections and exercises, you'll translate insights into action, creating lasting change in how you see yourself and navigate your professional world. The final section of the workbook helps you integrate all you've discovered and commit to your boldest vision for the future. But you can take notes anywhere—in a well-loved journal, on a spare piece of paper, on the inside cover of this book. Keep going until you've captured every drop of that dream, down to the most minute detail.

Feel free to map it all out on a vision board, using clippings from magazines, pages printed from the internet, or even your own drawings to capture what you want. Notice what you're drawn to and why.

Think about what it might mean for your life. Maybe that hobby or volunteer role is actually your calling, the thing that will ultimately get you out of bed in the morning. Maybe you're interested in going in a completely different direction. Or you've been headed the right way all along, but a few shifts will point you in a far more meaningful direction.

Remember that you're free to do it. **You get to step into your power and decide what you want for yourself, even if it feels scary.**

This is your narrative; this is your life. It's about what you want—and what you deserve. Don't hold back.

You can have it. You are powerful enough to create it, just as you are. In fact, you're more than enough.

And when you realize it, when you know it in your bones, that's when it starts to feel right. When everything is in alignment—your purpose, your values, your life and the people in it—things start to click. That's when you can move through the world with ease and grace. You level up. You reach a different plane. That's a whole different kind of existence, one bolstered by the love of countless supporters, mentors, sponsors, and role models all rooting for you—including me.

> The most powerful mirror, however, is the one you create for yourself through self-knowledge, environmental awareness, and strategic action.

The Mirror Effect: Reflecting Your True Power

Throughout this book, I've shared numerous stories of incredible leaders who have faced challenges similar to yours and found ways to overcome them. I've opened up about my own journey from self-doubt to self-assurance, from feeling like an imposter to knowing I belong at every table where decisions are made.

These stories serve as mirrors, reflecting possibilities that exist for you, too. When you see yourself in these narratives—in Maya's confrontation with misperception, in Irma's navigation of a toxic environment, in Liat's journey to claim her worth, in Em's transformation of their board—you glimpse your own potential.

The most powerful mirror, however, is the one you create for yourself through self-knowledge, environmental awareness, and strategic action. When you look into this mirror, you no longer see the limitations others have placed on you. Instead, you see your inherent worth, your unique talents, your boundless potential. In short, you see yourself as you truly are: powerful beyond measure.

And as you continue to grow and thrive, you **become a mirror for others.** Your courage inspires those around you. Your boundaries teach others what's acceptable. Your success demonstrates what's possible. This is the true Mirror Effect—the ripple of transformation that begins with you and extends outward, changing not just your life but the lives of everyone you touch.

With this book, I've tried to be a mirror for you: to reflect your potential and greatness with stories and strategies from my life and the people who have influenced me to become my full self. I hope you will embrace the opportunity to be that mirror too—to show the people in your life what they can become if only they step into their power and accept all that they were meant to be and all that they already are. The opportunity is two-fold to do right by the most important person of all in this journey—you—and teach others just how powerful they are if they can just recognize their own brilliance.

It's been such a blessing to be on this journey with you, and I'll continue to be here every step of the way. Together, we will create a world where all of us can step into our power, share our gifts, and thrive without compromise.

The world is waiting for the fully expressed version of you. It's time to spread your wings and fly.

ABOUT THE AUTHOR

SHEILA GUJRATHI, MD, is a biotech entrepreneur, executive, and champion for women and other underrepresented groups in leadership. Over the past 25 years, she's had the privilege of developing life-changing medicines for patients with serious diseases while building and running multiple biotech companies—including some pretty exciting exits along the way. She currently serves as a chairwoman, board director, strategic advisor, and consultant to many start-up companies and investment funds.

She has taken three biotech companies public and realized multi-billion-dollar acquisitions. Dr. Gujrathi was the co-founder and former CEO of Gossamer Bio and the former Chief Medical Officer of Receptos and has served on multiple company boards as either a Chairwoman or Director. She is currently back to founding and building several biotech companies where she focuses on developing meaningful therapies for patients with high unmet medical needs.

Her journey started at Northwestern University, where she earned both her M.D. and biomedical engineering degree in the accelerated honors program in medical education, and later took her from the academic halls of Harvard Medical School, UCSF, and Stanford to the corporate rooms of world-class companies like McKinsey & Company, Genentech, and Bristol Myers Squibb.

Dr. Gujrathi has earned multiple leadership awards, including AIMBE Fellow, BLOC100 Luminary, Corporate Directors Forum Director of the Year, Healthcare Technology Report Top 25 Women Leaders in Biotechnology, Athena Pinnacle Award, and Endpoints 20 Biopharm R&D and was named among the Fiercest Women in Life Sciences. But what really lights her up? Creating the kind of supportive, inclusive environments she wished she'd had throughout her career. That's why she co-founded the Biotech CEO Sisterhood, a group of transformative trailblazing female CEOs, and the South Asian Biopharma Alliance—because she believes we're all better when we lift each other up.

When she's not working to bring new therapies to patients or mentoring the next generation of leaders, you'll find her at home with her family, trying to keep up with her teenagers' latest adventures.

NOTES

Chapter 1

1   "KPMG Study Finds 75% of Executive Women Experience Imposter Syndrome." Info. kpmg.us. October 7, 2020. https://info.kpmg.us/news-perspectives/people-culture/kpmg-study-finds-most-female-executives-experience-imposter-syndrome.html.

2   Fyle, Sundiatu Dixon, Kevin Dolan, Vivian Hunt, and Sara Prince. "Diversity Wins: How Inclusion Matters." McKinsey & Company. May 19, 2020. https://www.mckinsey.com/featured-insights/diversity-and-inclusion/diversity-wins-how-inclusion-matters.

3   Gompers, Paul, and Silpa Kovvali. "The Other Diversity Dividend." *Harvard Business Review*. July 2018. https://hbr.org/2018/07/the-other-diversity-dividend.

4   Hinchliffe, Emma. "The Female CEOs on This Year's Fortune 500 Just Broke Three All-Time Records." *Fortune*. June 2, 2021. https://fortune.com/2021/06/02/female-ceos-fortune-500-2021-women-ceo-list-roz-brewer-walgreens-karen-lynch-cvs-thasunda-brown-duckett-tiaa/.

5   Minor, Maria. "Did You Know the Total Number of Female Chairs of the Board Are Less than Male Chairs Named John?" *Forbes*. December 21, 2020. https://www.forbes.com/sites/mariaminor/2020/12/21/did-you-know-the total-number-of-female-chairs-of-the-board-are-less-than-male-chairs-named-john/.

6   "Women in the Workplace 2022: The Full Report." Lean In. 2022. https://leanin.org/women-in-the-workplace-report-2022.

7   Schulz, Bailey. "Report Finds More Women Leaders Are Leaving Their Jobs. Here's Why." *USA Today*. October 19, 2022. https://www.usatoday.com/story/money/2022/10/19/women-leaders-leave-company-higher-rate/10532453002/.

8   "Still Struggling: Not Enough Women in the C-Suite." McKinsey & Company. October 15, 2020. https://www.mckinsey.com/featured-insights/sustainable-inclusive-growth/chart-of-the-day/still-struggling-not-enough-women-in-the-c-suite.

9   Treisman, Rachel. "Women Leaders Switch Jobs at Record Rates as They Demand Better from Their Workplaces." NPR. October 28, 2022. https://www.npr.org/2022/10/28/1132232414/women-workforce-switching-jobs.

10   "Being Black in Corporate America: An Intersectional Exploration." Coqual. n.d. https://coqual.org/reports/being-black-in-corporate-america-an-intersectional-exploration/.

11   Xintian Tina Wang. "Over Half of Women Experience Microaggressions at Work. Here's How to Push Back." Inc.com. October 26, 2022. https://www.inc.com/xintian-tina-wang/microaggression-integrating-women-leaders-workplace-equity.html.

12   Alinor, Malissa. "Research: The Real-Time Impact of Microaggressions." *Harvard Business Review*. May 17, 2022. https://hbr.org/2022/05/research-the-real-time-impact-of-microaggressions.

13   LaHucik, Kyle. "'Banding together': 50 female biotech executives lay out plans for board diversity, new companies, and mentoring founders." EndPoints News. March 22, 2023. https://endpoints.news/banding-together-50-female-biotech-executives-lay-out-plans-for-board-diversity-new-companies-and-mentoring-founders/.

Chapter 2

1   "Trauma." Administration for Children and Families. https://www.acf.hhs.gov/trauma-toolkit/trauma-concept.

2   Gervais, Michael. *The First Rule of Mastery: Stop Worrying about What People Think of You*. HBR Store. 2025. https://store.hbr.org/product/the-first-rule-of-mastery-stop-worrying-about-what-people-think-of-you/.

3   Carter, Christine Michel. "Fear, Distress, and Safety: Companies Trigger a Fight-or-Flight Response in Female Talent." *Forbes*. September 29, 2022. https://www.forbes.com/sites/christinecarter/2022/09/29/fear-distress-and-safety-companies-trigger-a-fight-or-flight-response-in-female-talent/.

4   Timm, Tricia Montalvo. "The Perfectionism Pitfall: Why It Holds Women Leaders Back and How to Break the Cycle." Chief. October 19, 2023. https://chief.com/articles/the-perfectionism-pitfall-why-it-holds-women-leaders-back-and-how-to-break-the-cycle.

5   Byng, Rhonesha. "Failure Is Not an Option: The Pressure Black Women Feel to Succeed." *Forbes*. August 31, 2017. https://www.forbes.com/sites/rhoneshabyng/2017/08/31/failure-is-not-an-option-the-pressure-black-women-feel-to-succeed/.

6   Shmalz, Fred. "3 Tips for Conquering Self-Doubt at Work." Kellogg Insight. August 21, 2020. https://insight.kellogg.northwestern.edu/article/3-tips-conquer-self-doubt-at-work.

7   Alexander, Khera. "Ambitious Women: Almost 90% Globally Are Penalized at Work — Women of Influence." Women of Influence+. March 1, 2023. https://www.womenofinfluence.ca/2023/03/01/tps-press-release/.

8   Barrall, Suzanne. "Shame vs. Guilt." BreneBrown.com. January 15, 2013. https://brenebrown.com/articles/2013/01/15/shame-v-guilt.

9   Jantz, Gregory L. "Identifying the Root Causes of Shame." *Psychology Today*. September 22, 2022. https://www.psychologytoday.com/us/blog/hope-relationships/202209/identifying-the-root-causes-shame.

10   Brach, Tara. "Article: Awakening from the Trance of Unworthiness." TaraBrach.com. July 1, 2011. https://www.tarabrach.com/inquiring-trance/.

11   "About Catalyst." Catalyst. https://www.catalyst.org/mission/.

12   "Do the Work." The Work of Byron Katie. n.d. https://thework.com/instruction-the-work-byron-katie/.

Chapter 3

1   Villines, Zawn. "People Pleaser: Definition, Signs, Risks, and How to Stop." Medical News Today. May 27, 2022. https://www.medicalnewstoday.com/articles/people-pleaser.

2   "People-Pleasing." *Psychology Today*. n.d. https://www.psychologytoday.com/us/basics/people-pleasing.

3   Stillman, Jessica. "Want to Be a Great Leader? Stop Being Nice and Start Being Kind." Inc. January 29, 2021. https://www.inc.com/jessica-stillman/kindness-leadership-ethics-santa-clara-university.html.

4   Johnston, Oliver. "The Difference Between Being Nice and Being Kind." Project Happiness. n.d. https://shop.projecthappiness.org/blogs/project-happiness/the-difference-between-being-nice-and-being-kind.

5   Haas, Susan Biali. "How to Stop People-Pleasing." *Psychology Today*. October 11, 2013. https://www.psychologytoday.com/us/blog/prescriptions-for-life/201310/how-to-stop-people-pleasing.

6   DeVee, Gina. The Audacity to Be Queen. Legacy Lit. 2020.

7   "Definition of SYNDROME." Merriam-Webster.com. 2019. https://www.merriam-webster.com/dictionary/syndrome.

8   "Definition of IMPOSTER SYNDROME." Merriam-Webster.com. 2020. https://www.merriam-webster.com/dictionary/imposter%20syndrome.

9   "Imposter Syndrome." *Psychology Today*. 2019. https://www.psychologytoday.com/us/basics/imposter-syndrome.

10 Tulshyan, Ruchika, and Jodi-Ann Burey. "Stop Telling Women They Have Imposter Syndrome." *Harvard Business Review*. February 11, 2021. https://hbr.org/2021/02/stop-telling-women-they-have-imposter-syndrome.

11 Paulise, Luciana. "75% of Women Executives Experience Imposter Syndrome in the Workplace." *Forbes*. March 8, 2023. https://www.forbes.com/sites/lucianapaulise/2023/03/08/75-of-women-executives-experience-imposter-syndrome-in-the-workplace/.

12 Aragão, Carolina. "Gender Pay Gap in U.S. Hasn't Changed Much in Two Decades." Pew Research Center. March 1, 2023. https://www.pewresearch.org/short-reads/2023/03/01/gender-pay-gap-facts/.

13 Cuncic, Arlin. "Imposter Syndrome: Why You May Feel like a Fraud." Verywell Mind. September 23, 2024. https://www.verywellmind.com/imposter-syndrome-and-social-anxiety-disorder-4156469.

14 Rickey Smiley. "Michelle Obama Speaks About Imposter Syndrome." YouTube. May 18, 2019. https://www.youtube.com/watch?v=Rta_mOWsF8s.

15 "Where will you find your next leader?" EY and ESPNW. 2015. https://www.sportknowhowxl.nl/files/2023/ey-where-will-you-find-your-next-leader-1.pdf.

16 Brown, Paul B. "'You Miss 100% of the Shots You Don't Take.' You Need to Start Shooting at Your Goals." *Forbes*. January 12, 2014. https://www.forbes.com/sites/actiontrumpseverything/2014/01/12/you-miss-100-of-the-shots-you-dont-take-so-start-shooting-at-your-goal/.

17 Bartlett, Steven. 2022. "How I Taught Millions of Women the Most Important Skill: Girls Who Code Founder Reshma Saujani." The Diary of CEO with Steven Bartlett. June 6, 2022. https://www.youtube.com/watch?v=SgPVgPYnT_M.

18 "Founder, Partner." OpenView. 2019. https://openviewpartners.com/author/scott-maxwell/.

19 Henni, Janine. "Meghan Markle Says 'Difficult' Is 'Code Word for the B-Word' in Latest Podcast Episode." People.com. November 8, 2022. https://people.com/royals/meghan-markle-releases-latest-episode-archetypes-podcast-on-b-word/.

20 "Boss Bitch." Nicole Lapin. July 6, 2023. https://nicolelapin.com/boss-bitch/.

21 "Workplace Discrimination: Women in Power—Assertive or Aggressive?" Mercuryclothiers.com. April 24, 2020. https://mercuryclothiers.com/workplace-discrimination/.

22 Wilkie, Dana. "Let It Go: Teaching a Micromanager How to Chill." SHRM. March 31, 2020. https://www.shrm.org/resourcesandtools/hr-topics/employee-relations/pages/micro-managers.aspx.

23 Molinsky, Andy. "How to Stop Being Such a Micromanager." *Psychology Today*. February 26, 2018. https://www.psychologytoday.com/us/blog/adaptation/201802/how-stop-being-such-Micromanager.

24 Lebow, Hilary I. "How to Stop Being a People-Pleaser (but Still Be You)." Psych Central. July 20, 2021. https://psychcentral.com/health/tips-to-stop-being-a-people-pleaser.

25 Hinchliffe, Emma, and Devin Hance. "Powerful Women's Secret to the Power Pose? 'Just Take up Space.'" *Fortune*. March 8, 2019. https://fortune.com/2019/03/08/international-womens-day-power-poses/.

26 Garvin, Lia. "How to Stop Micromanaging and Start Empowering." *Harvard Business Review*. September 9, 2022. https://hbr.org/2022/09/how-to-stop-micromanaging-and-start-empowering.

Chapter 4

1 Grady, Constance. "Why Marianne Williamson's Most Famous Passage Keeps Getting Cited as a Nelson Mandela Quote." Vox. July 30, 2019. https://www.vox.com/culture/2019/7/30/20699833/marianne-williamson-our-deepest-fear-nelson-mandela-return-to-love.

2 Khazan, Olga. "Forget Self-Esteem—Try Self-Compassion Instead." *Atlantic*. May 6, 2016. https://www.theatlantic.com/health/archive/2016/05/why-self-compassion-works-better-than-self-esteem/481473/.

3 Neff, Kristin. "Exercise 6: Self-Compassion Journal." Self-Compassion. February 23, 2015. https://self-compassion.org/exercise-6-self-compassion-journal/.

4 Ibid.

5 Ibid.

6 Therapy in a Nutshell. "Intrusive Thoughts and Overthinking: The Skill of Cognitive Defusion 20/30." YouTube. https://www.youtube.com/watch?v=V3vhXQy48jo.

7 Chiu, Allyson. "How to Make Self-Affirmation Work, Based on Science." *Washington Post*. May 2, 2022. https://www.washingtonpost.com/wellness/2022/05/02/do-self-affir-mations-work/.

8 Cohen, G. L., Julio Garcia, Nancy Apfel, and Allison Master. "Reducing the Racial Achievement Gap: A Social-Psychological Intervention." *Science* 313, no. 5791 (2006): 1307–10. https://doi.org/10.1126/science.1128317.

9 Powell, Alvin. "Harvard Researchers Study How Mindfulness May Change the Brain in Depressed Patients." *Harvard Gazette*. April 9, 2018. https://news.harvard.edu/gazette/story/2018/04/harvard-researchers-study-how-mindfulness-may-change-the-brain-in-depressed-patients.

10 Exley, Christine, and Judd Kessler. "Why Don't Women Self-Promote as Much as Men?" *Harvard Business Review*. December 19, 2019. https://hbr.org/2019/12/why-dont-women-self-promote-as-much-as-men.

11 Miller, Jo. "The Soul-Crushing Truth About Women and Self-Promotion." *Forbes*. April 29, 2021. https://www.forbes.com/sites/jomiller/2021/04/29/the-soul-crushing-truth-about-women-and-self-promotion/?sh=4669b6d86906.

12 Wayne, Sandy J., Jiaqing Sun, Donald H. Kluemper, Gordon W. Cheung, and Adaora Ubaka. "The Cost of Managing Impressions for Black Employees: An Expectancy Violation Theory Perspective." *Journal of Applied Psychology* 108 (2). https://doi.org/10.1037/apl0001030.

13 Winfrey, Oprah. "Oprah Asks, Are You Enough for Yourself?" Oprah Daily. March 12, 2023. https://www.oprahdaily.com/life/a43279495/oprah-meant-to-be-intention/.

14 Harvard Health Publishing. "Yoga—Benefits Beyond the Mat." Harvard Health. September 8, 2021. https://www.health.harvard.edu/staying-healthy/yoga-benefits-beyond-the-mat.

15 "Morning Pages." Juliacameronlive.com. n.d. https://juliacameronlive.com/basic-tools/morning-pages/.

16 "The Miracle of the Artist's Date." Juliacameronlive.com. 2025. https://juliacameronlive.com/book/the-miracle-of-the-artists-date/.

17 Centers for Disease Control and Prevention. "Benefits of Physical Activity." Centers for Disease Control and Prevention. August 1, 2023. https://www.cdc.gov/physicalactivity/basics/pa-health/index.htm.

Chapter 5

1 Harter, Jim, and Amy Adkins. "Employees Want a Lot More from Their Managers." Gallup. April 8, 2015. https://www.gallup.com/workplace/236570/employees-lot-managers.aspx.

2 "Does Fear Motivate Workers—or Make Things Worse?" 2018. Knowledge at Wharton. December 4, 2018. https://knowledge.wharton.upenn.edu/podcast/knowledge-at-wharton-podcast/fear-motivate-workers-make-things-worse/.

3 Shedletzky, Stephen. 2023. *Speak-Up Culture*. Page Two.

4 Gallo, Amy. "What Is Psychological Safety?" *Harvard Business Review*. February 15, 2023. https://hbr.org/2023/02/what-is-psychological-safety.

5 Bresman, Henrik, and Amy C. Edmondson. "Research: To Excel, Diverse Teams Need Psychological Safety." *Harvard Business Review*. March 17, 2022. https://hbr.org/2022/03/research-to-excel-diverse-teams-need-psychological-safety.

6 "Just 26 percent of leaders create psychological safety for their teams." McKinsey & Company. February 24, 2021. https://www.mckinsey.com/featured-insights/sustainable-inclusive-growth/charts/just-26-percent-of-leaders-create-psychological-safety-for-their-teams.

7 Cespedes, Frank V. "Stop Using Battle Metaphors in Your Company Strategy." *Harvard Business Review*. December 19, 2014. https://hbr.org/2014/12/stop-using-battle-metaphors-in-your-company-strategy.

8 Expert panel. "Eight Ways to Foster Healthy Competition Among Your Team Members." *Forbes*. July 27, 2022. https://www.forbes.com/councils/theyec/2022/07/27/eight-ways-to-foster-healthy-competition-among-your-team-members/.

9 White, Doug and Polly. "5 Ways to Promote Healthy Competition." *Entrepreneur*. April 11, 2017. https://www.entrepreneur.com/leadership/5-ways-to-promote-healthy-competition/292628.

10 Abbajay, Mary. "Ask an Expert: What Should I Do If My Boss Is Gaslighting Me?" *Harvard Business Review*. November 6, 2020. https://hbr.org/2020/11/ask-an-expert-what-should-i-do-if-my-boss-is-gaslighting-me.

11 Somers, Meredith. "Women Are Less Likely than Men to Be Promoted. Here's One Reason Why." MIT Sloan School of Management. April 12, 2022. https://mitsloan.mit.edu/ideas-made-to-matter/women-are-less-likely-men-to-be-promoted-heres-one-reason-why.

12 Ni, Preston. "7 Signs of Gaslighting at the Workplace." July 19, 2020. *Psychology Today*. https://www.psychologytoday.com/us/blog/communication-success/202007/7-signs-of-gaslighting-at-the-workplace.

13 Waters, Shonna. "What Is Gaslighting at Work? 6 Signs of Gaslighting and How to Deal." BetterUp. December 22, 2021. https://www.betterup.com/blog/gaslighting-at-work.

14 Blair, Sonia. 2021. "Tall Poppy Syndrome and Its Effects on Our Closest Relationships." *Harper's Bazaar Australia*. October 5, 2021. https://harpersbazaar.com.au/tall-poppy-syndrome-wellbeing-mental-health/.

Chapter 6

1   Graham, Luke. "Four Warning Signs of a Workplace Tyrant and What to Do About It."
    May 31, 2018. LinkedIn. https://www.linkedin.com/pulse/four-warning-signs-workplace-
    tyrant-what-do-luke-graham/.
2   "Disability Discrimination." US EEOC. n.d. https://www.eeoc.gov/youth/disability-dis-
    crimination.
3   Akerlof, George A., and Rachel E. Kranton. 2000. "Economics and Identity." *Quarterly
    Journal of Economics*. 115, no. 3 (2022): 715–753. http://public.econ.duke.edu/~rek8/eco-
    nomicsandidentity.pdf.
4   "Where will you find your next leader?"
5   Randall, Jason. "Imposter Syndrome Affects the Highest-Level Competitors in Sports
    and Business." *Forbes*. April 22, 2022. https://www.forbes.com/sites/forbesbooksau-
    thors/2022/04/22/imposter-syndrome-affects-the-highest-level-competitors-in-sports-and-
    business/.
6   Marcus, Bonnie. "The Dark Side of Female Rivalry in the Workplace and What to Do About
    It." *Forbes*. January 13, 2016. https://www.forbes.com/sites/bonniemarcus/2016/01/13/
    the-dark-side-of-female-Rivalry-in-the-workplace-and-what-to-do-about-it/.
7   Huizen, Jennifer. "What Is Gaslighting? Examples and How to Respond." Medical News
    Today. March 22, 2024. https://www.medicalnewstoday.com/articles/gaslighting.

Chapter 7

1   "Unconscious Bias." Vanderbilt University. December 19, 2016. https://www.vanderbilt.
    edu/diversity/unconscious-bias/.
2   Team Asana. "19 Unconscious Bias Examples and How to Prevent Them." Asana. May 17,
    2021. https://asana.com/resources/unconscious-bias-examples.
3   "The Science of Bias." Smithsonian. n.d. https://biasinsideus.si.edu/online-exhibition/the-
    science-of-bias.
4   Ibid.
5   Ricee, Susanne. "What Is Affinity Bias?." Diversity.com. July 13, 2023. https://diversity.
    social/affinity-bias-definition/.
6   Davis, Jeffrey. "The Bias Against Difference." *Psychology Today*. June 25, 2020. https://
    www.psychologytoday.com/us/blog/tracking-wonder/202006/the-bias-against-difference.
7   "Understanding Implicit Bias." Kirwaninstitute.osu.edu. May 29, 2012. https://kirwanin-
    stitute.osu.edu/article/understanding-implicit-bias.
8   Motro, Daphna, Jonathan B. Evans, Aleksander P. J. Ellis, and Lehman Benson III. "The
    'Angry Black Woman' Stereotype at Work." *Harvard Business Review*. January 31, 2022.
    https://hbr.org/2022/01/the-angry-black-woman-stereotype-at-work.
9   "4 Common Ethnic & Cultural Stereotypes in the Workplace." EasyLlama. n.d. https://
    www.easyllama.com/blog/4-common-ethnic-and-cultural-stereotypes-in-the-workplace/.
10 Hassan, Adeel. "Confronting Asian-American Stereotypes." *New York Times*. June 23,
    2018. https://www.nytimes.com/2018/06/23/us/confronting-asian-american-stereotypes.
    html.
11 Leonard, Bill. "Study Suggests Bias Against 'Black' Names on Resumes." SHRM. February
    1, 2003. https://www.shrm.org/hr-today/news/hr-magazine/pages/0203hrnews2.aspx.
12 Young, Robin, and Serena McMahon. "Name Discrimination Study Finds Lakisha and Ja-
    mal Still Less Likely to Get Hired than Emily and Greg." WBUR. August 18, 2021. https://
    www.wbur.org/hereandnow/2021/08/18/name-discrimination-jobs.
13 Papillon, Kimberly. "Two Types of Bias." Georgetown.edu. 2019. https://nccc.georgetown.
    edu/bias/module-3/1.php.

14 "Op-Ed: Technology and Gender Equality—Bringing Women and Girls to the Centre of Innovation." UN Women—Headquarters. n.d. https://www.unwomen.org/en/news-stories/op-ed/2023/03/op-ed-technology-and-gender-equality-bringing-women-and-girls-to-the-centre-of-innovation.

15 "Innovation and Technology for Gender Equality." UNICEF. n.d. https://www.unicef.org/eap/innovation-and-technology-gender-equality.

16 "DigitALL: Innovation and Technology for Gender Equality." World Bank Blogs. 2023. https://blogs.worldbank.org/youth-transforming-africa/digitall-innovation-and-technology-gender-equality.

Chapter 8

1   Lencioni, Patrick. "Make Your Values Mean Something." *Harvard Business Review*. July 2002. https://hbr.org/2002/07/make-your-values-mean-something.

2   Naber, Andrew. "One Third of Your Life Is Spent at Work." Gettysburg College. 2021. https://www.gettysburg.edu/news/stories?id=79db7b34-630c-4f49-ad32-4ab9ea48e72b.

3   Stahl, Ashley. "3 Benefits of Diversity in the Workplace." *Forbes*. December 17, 2021. https://www.forbes.com/sites/ashleystahl/2021/12/17/3-benefits-of-diversity-in-the-workplace/.

4   Rogers, Kristie. "Do Your Employees Feel Respected?" *Harvard Business Review*. July 2018. https://hbr.org/2018/07/do-your-employees-feel-respected.

5   "What Is Psychological Safety?" McKinsey & Company. 2023. https://www.mckinsey.com/featured-insights/mckinsey-explainers/what-is-psychological-safety.

6   Ibid.

7   "How Much of Communication Is Nonverbal?" University of Texas, Permian Basin. November 3, 2020. https://online.utpb.edu/about-us/articles/communication/how-much-of-communication-is-nonverbal/.

8   "Mirroring in Interviews and the Workplace." Indeed.com. 2024. https://www.indeed.com/hire/c/info/mirroring-in-interviews-and-workplace.

9   Patagonia. "Our Footprint." Patagonia. 2025. https://www.patagonia.com/our-footprint/.

10 Anderson, Bruce. "5 'Ridiculous' Ways Patagonia Has Built a Culture That Does Well and Does Good." LinkedIn. September 27, 2019. https://www.linkedin.com/business/talent/blog/talent-connect/ways-patagonia-built-ridiculous-culture.

11 Gelles, David. "Billionaire No More: Patagonia Founder Gives Away the Company." *New York Times*. September 14, 2022. https://www.nytimes.com/2022/09/14/climate/patagonia-climate-philanthropy-chouinard.html.

12 Hilton. "Hilton Ranked #2 Workplace in the World." Stories from Hilton. October 13, 2022. https://stories.hilton.com/releases/hilton-ranked-2-workplace-in-the-world.

13 "Fortune Best Workplaces for Women™ 2022." Great Place to Work®. 2022. https://www.greatplacetowork.com/best-workplaces/women/2022.

14 "Hilton Worldwide Holdings | 2021 100 Best Companies." *Fortune*. 2022. https://fortune.com/company/hilton-worldwide-holdings/best-companies/.

15 Batchelor, Marlena. "Inside the World's 15 Best Female-Friendly Companies to Work For." January 21, 2023. *CEO Magazine*. https://www.theceomagazine.com/business/management-leadership/best-workplaces-for-women/.

16 Workhuman. "7 Companies with Great Culture in 2022–Plus, How 5 Organizations Went from Bad to Good." Workhuman. October 30, 2022. https://www.workhuman.com/blog/companies-with-great-culture/.

17 Loescher, Kathleen. "Cisco Is #1 on Fortune's 100 Best Companies to Work For® in the U.S. List—Again!" Cisco Blogs. April 4, 2023. https://blogs.cisco.com/wearecisco/cisco-is-1-on-fortunes-100-best-companies-to-work-for-in-the-u-s-list-again.

Chapter 9

1   Wilkie, Dana. "How DE&I Evolved in the C-Suite." SHRM. July 1, 2022. https://www.shrm.org/executive/resources/articles/pages/evolving-executive-dei-diversity-c-suite.aspx.

2   Frumin, Aliyah. "Ageism in the Workplace Affects Women at Every Stage of Their Career: Study." Ampproject.org. MSNBC. July 14, 2023. https://www-msnbc-com.cdn.ampproject.org/c/s/www.msnbc.com/msnbc/amp/ncna1306729.

3   Ibid.

4   Ibid.

5   Chane, Dianna. "The Power of Female Mentors: Why We Need More Women Leading Today's Workforce." *Forbes*. February 10, 2020. https://www.forbes.com/sites/forbesbusinesscouncil/2020/02/10/the-power-of-female-mentors-why-we-need-more-women-leading-todays-workforce.

6   Avlani, Shrenik. "Why women need to build networking circles." April 29, 2024. Mint Hyderabad. https://www.pressreader.com/india/mint-hyderabad/20240429/282265260499329?srsltid=AfmBOoqtch8SSE6VF7jFjf1CSbrmLiafRohCsHddKQcr5OPIR1F6-urA.

7   Ibid.

8   Ibid.

9   Ibid.

10   Berk, Christina Cheddar. "Having a Woman in the Boardroom or C-Suite Drives Even Wider Diversity, Study Finds." CNBC. July 28, 2022. https://www.cnbc.com/2022/07/28/having-women-in-the-boardroom-or-c-suite-drives-diversity-study-finds.html.

11   Avlani. "Why women need to build networking circles."

12   Ibid.

13   Comaford, Christine. 2019. "76% of People Think Mentors Are Important, but Only 37% Have One." *Forbes*. July 3, 2019. https://www.forbes.com/sites/christinecomaford/2019/07/03/new-study-76-of-people-think-mentors-are-important-but-only-37-have-one.

14   "Givers vs. Takers: The Surprising Truth About Who Gets Ahead." n.d. Knowledge at Wharton. https://knowledge.wharton.upenn.edu/podcast/knowledge-at-wharton-podcast/givers-vs-takers-the-surprising-truth-about-who-gets-ahead/.

15   Ibid.

16   Ibid.

17   Ibid.

Chapter 10

1   "Women Don't Ask: Negotiation and the Gender Divide." UC Davis. n.d. https://ucd-advance.ucdavis.edu/post/women-dont-ask-negotiation-and-gender-divide.

2   Ibid.

3   Emerson, Mary Sharp. 2022. "Women Negotiation Skills." Professional Development | Harvard DCE. July 28, 2022. https://professional.dce.harvard.edu/blog/women-negotiation-skills-how-women-can-get-what-they-want-in-a-negotiation/.

4   Bowles, Hannah Riley. 2014. "Why Women Don't Negotiate Their Job Offers." *Harvard Business Review*. June 19, 2014. https://hbr.org/2014/06/why-women-dont-negotiate-their-job-offers.

5   "Women Don't Ask: Negotiation and the Gender Divide."

6   "Women Don't Ask: Negotiation and the Gender Divide."

7   Swaminathan, Aarthi. "The Key Reasons Why Women Don't Negotiate Their Salary." Yahoo Finance. March 8, 2019. https://finance.yahoo.com/news/women-salary-negotiation-huffpost-050000019.html.

8   "Men Are Promoted More Often than Women at Entry Level—Even Though Women Have More College Degrees." n.d. Lean In. https://leanin.org/women-in-the-workplace/2019/progress-at-the-top.

9   Elsesser, Kim. "Why Women Fall Short in Negotiations (It's Not Lack of Skill)." *Forbes*. January 21, 2021. https://www.forbes.com/sites/kimelsesser/2021/01/21/why-women-fall-short-in-negotiations-its-not-lack-of-skill/?sh=18fcc9ba5d02.

10   Ibid.

11   Bowles. "Why Women Don't Negotiate Their Job Offers."

12   Elsesser. "Why Women Fall Short in Negotiations (It's Not Lack of Skill)."

13   Bowles. "Why Women Don't Negotiate Their Job Offers."

14   Ibid.

15   Ibid.

16   Ibid.

17   Ibid.

18   PON Staff. "Counteracting Racial and Gender Bias in Job Negotiations." PON–Program on Negotiation at Harvard Law School. December 31, 2018. https://www.pon.harvard.edu/daily/leadership-skills-daily/counteracting-racial-and-gender-bias-in-job-negotiations-nb/.

19   Ibid.

20   Ibid.

21   Ibid.

22   Ibid.

23   Purushothaman, Deepa, Deborah M. Kolb, Hannah Riley Bowles, and Valerie Purdie-Greenaway. "Negotiating as a Woman of Color." *Harvard Business Review*, January 14, 2022. https://hbr.org/2022/01/negotiating-as-a-woman-of-color.

24   Ibid.

25   Ibid.

26   Kolb, Deborah M. "A Short Course from Howard Raiffa." *Negotiation Journal* 33, no. 4 (2017): 333–35. https://doi.org/10.1111/nejo.12193.

27   Ibid.

28   Ibid.

29   "How Women Can Negotiate for More." Lean In. 2024. https://leanin.org/negotiation#.

30   Purushothaman, Kolb, Bowles, and Purdie-Greenaway. "Negotiating as a Woman of Color."

31   Ibid.

32   Iacurci, Greg. "Pay Secrecy Norms Have 'Simply Lost Their Teeth,' Say Experts. Here's Why." CNBC. September 18, 2023. https://www.cnbc.com/2023/09/18/why-pay-transparency-is-on-the-rise-for-jobseekers.html.

33   Obloj, Tomasz, and Todd Zenger. "Research: The Complicated Effects of Pay Transparency." *Harvard Business Review*. February 8, 2023. https://hbr.org/2023/02/research-the-complicated-effects-of-pay-transparency.

34   Ibid.

35   Obloj, Tomasz, and Todd Zenger. "The Influence of Pay Transparency on (Gender) Inequity, Inequality and the Performance Basis of Pay." *Nature Human Behaviour* 6 (February). https://doi.org/10.1038/s41562-022-01288-9.

36   Obloj and Zenger. "Research: The Complicated Effects of Pay Transparency."

Chapter 11

1   "Flow." n.d. *Psychology Today*. https://www.psychologytoday.com/us/basics/flow.

2   HannahWadFans. "Ted Lasso–Rebecca Calms Her Anxiety." YouTube. May 18, 2023. https://www.youtube.com/watch?v=S503PzZoQBg.

3   Carney, Dana R., Amy J. C. Cuddy, and Andy J. Yap. "Power Posing: Brief Nonverbal Displays Affect Neuroendocrine Levels and Risk Tolerance." *Psychological Science* 21, no. 10 (2010): 1363–68. https://doi.org/10.1177/0956797610383437.
4   Schütz, Astrid. "88 Studies of Power Poses Reveal Whether They Work or Not." *Fast Company*. June 12, 2022. https://www.fastcompany.com/90760166/88-studies-of-power-poses-reveal-whether-they-work-or-not.
5   Ibid.
6   Tony Robbins. "Harvard Study on Power Postures." YouTube. May 30, 2023. https://www.youtube.com/watch?v=7RvIjmNVdcE.
7   Ibid.